The Wedding of

_____

&

_____

on

_____

A Personal Wedding Planner

Sharon Capen Cook
and
Elizabeth Gale

Adams Media Corporation
Avon, Massachusetts

Published by
Adams Media Corporation
57 Littlefield Street, Avon MA 02322. U.S.A.
www.adamsmedia.com

ISBN: 1-58062-795-1
Second Edition

Printed in China through Palace Press International.

J I H G F E D C B

FRONT COVER PHOTOGRAPH ©2001 Claudia Kunin/Corbis
INTERIOR PHOTO CREDITS:
brand X pictures, page 139(b-l, b-r)
Comstock, Inc., page 106(t)
Corbis ©2001, page 11, 12(t-l, t-r, b), 37, 39(t-r), 41(b-r), 42, 103, 104, 105(t-l, t-r, b), 106 (b),
139(t-r), 159(t, b-l), 162(t, b), 163(t-l, b), 164, 192(t, b), rear cover(b)
Eyewire ©2000, page 2, 39(t-l, b-r), 40, 41(m-l, t-r), 159 (b-r), 163(t-r), rear cover(t)
FPG International Corporation, page 161(t-l)
H. Armstrong Roberts, page 140(b)
The Image Bank, Inc., page 39(b-l), 41(b-l), 140(t-l, t-r), 191
International Photography LTD., page 139(t-l), 161(b)
Paula Cutone, page 161(t-r)
The Stock Market, page 38(t-l, t-r, b), 41(t-l), 160

Introduction

Planning your wedding can be as much fun as the wedding itself! Here's an all-in-one personal organizer that helps you set up everything for the celebration of a lifetime. . . and plan the wedding *your* way.

From selecting the invitations to choosing the attire, from setting the guest list to sharing the perfect honeymoon, *A Personal Wedding Planner* covers all the essentials. This book features a summary of all important deadlines, eighteen detailed chapters (featuring worksheets on all aspects of the wedding plan), and a pocket organizer for forms, notes, and receipts.

Use this book to organize, schedule, keep track of the details, and save time. You will find dozens of easy-to-use worksheets, important checklists, and a convenient set of calendar / reminders.

There's also advice on how you can add your own personal touch to all aspects of your wedding celebration, including floral arrangements, music, your choice of wedding vows, the sequence of your ceremony, and much, much more.

In short, *A Personal Wedding Planner* will help you customize the perfect wedding . . . yours. It makes a great keepsake, too!

E.G.
S.C.C.

Contents

TIME & MONEY

FAMILY, FRIENDS, & FINERY

FLOWERS, MUSIC, & MORE

CEREMONY

RECEPTION

HONEYMOON

Time & Money

Chapter One: Your Wedding Calendar

Planning the wedding can be exciting—and challenging! The guidelines below will help you make sense of the many deadlines you will face as you approach the organization of your wedding.

(Helpful hint: use a pencil rather than a pen as you fill in your own dates on the enclosed calendar sheets.)

> *Because you're likely to come back to this section again and again, we've placed it at the front of the book for easy reference.*

Six to twelve months before the wedding

1. Decide type of wedding
2. Decide time of day
3. Decide location
4. Set a date
5. Set a budget
6. Select bridal party
7. Plan color scheme
8. Select and order bridal gown
9. Select and order headpiece
10. Select and order shoes
11. Select and order attendants' gowns
12. Start honeymoon plans
13. Go to bridal gift registry
14. Start compiling the guest list
15. Select caterer
16. Select musicians
17. Select florist

He brought me to the banqueting house,
and his banner over me was love. —SONG OF SONGS 2:4 (RSV)

18. Select photographer
19. Announce engagement
20. Start planning reception
21. Reserve hall, hotel, etc., for reception
22. Plan to attend pre-marriage counseling at your church, if applicable
23. Select and order wedding rings

Three months before the wedding

1. Complete the guest list
2. Make doctor's appointments
3. Plan to have mothers select attire
4. Select and order invitations
5. Start compiling trousseau
6. Order personal stationery
7. Finalize reception arrangements (rent items now)
8. Make reservations for honeymoon
9. Confirm dress delivery
10. Confirm time and date with florist
11. Confirm time and date with caterer
12. Confirm time and date with photographer
13. Confirm time and date with musician
14. Confirm time and date with church
15. Discuss transportation to ceremony and reception
16. Select and order attire for groomsmen
17. Schedule bridesmaids' dress and shoe fittings

Two months before the wedding

1. Mail all invitations to allow time for R.S.V.P.'s
2. Order cake

To be loved, be lovable. —OVID

3. Arrange for appointment to get marriage license
4. Finalize honeymoon arrangements

One month before the wedding

1. Schedule bridal portrait
2. Reserve accommodations for guests
3. Begin to record gifts received and send thank you notes
4. Plan rehearsal and rehearsal dinner
5. Purchase gifts for bridal party
6. Purchase gift for fiancé if gifts are being exchanged
7. Schedule final fittings including accessories and shoes
8. Schedule appointments at beauty salon for attendants
9. Schedule bridesmaids' luncheon or party
10. Arrange for placement of guest book
11. Obtain wedding props, e.g. pillow for ring bearer, candles, etc.

Two weeks before the wedding

1. Mail bridal portrait with announcement to newspaper
2. Finalize wedding day transportation
3. Arrange to change name on license, Social Security card, etc.
4. Get marriage license
5. Confirm accommodations for guests
6. Prepare wedding announcements to be mailed after the wedding

One week before the wedding

1. Start packing for honeymoon
2. Finalize number of guests with caterer
3. Double check professional services—photographer, etc.
4. Plan seating arrangements
5. Confirm desired pictures with photographer

When two people are at one in their inmost hearts, they shatter even the strength of iron or of bronze. —I CHING

6. Style your hair with headpiece

7. Practice applying cosmetics in proper light

8. Arrange for one last fitting of all wedding attire

9. Make sure rings are picked up and fit properly

10. Confirm receipt of marriage license

11. Rehearsal/rehearsal dinner (one or two days before wedding)

Your wedding day

1. Try to relax and pamper yourself—take a long bath, have a manicure, etc.

2. Eat at least one small meal

3. Have your hair and make-up done a few hours before ceremony

4. Start dressing one to two hours before ceremony

5. Have photographer and attendants arrive two hours before ceremony if there are to be pre-wedding pictures

6. Arrange for music to start one-half hour prior to ceremony

7. Have mother of the groom seated five minutes before ceremony

8. Have mother of the bride seated immediately before processional

9. Arrange for the aisle runner to be rolled out by the ushers immediately before the processional

---

True love is a durable fire in the mind ever burning. —SIR WALTER RALEIGH

On this and following pages you will find a number of blank calendars for planning and customizing your wedding schedule. Along the left-hand side of each monthly calendar is a convenient quick-summary line for you to use for your first draft, and for important deadlines.

Your Wedding Planning Calendar

Seven to twelve months before the wedding

Month	Items to do

Your Wedding Planning Calendar
Six months before the wedding

	SUNDAY	MONDAY	TUESDAY
1			
2			
3			
4			
5			
6			
7			
8			
9			
10			
11			
12			
13			
14			
15			
16			
17			
18			
19			
20			
21			
22			
23			
24			
25			
26			
27			
28			
29			
30			
31			

Month _____

WEDNESDAY	THURSDAY	FRIDAY	SATURDAY

Your Wedding Planning Calendar
Five months before the wedding

	SUNDAY	MONDAY	TUESDAY
1			
2			
3			
4			
5			
6			
7			
8			
9			
10			
11			
12			
13			
14			
15			
16			
17			
18			
19			
20			
21			
22			
23			
24			
25			
26			
27			
28			
29			
30			
31			

Month

WEDNESDAY	THURSDAY	FRIDAY	SATURDAY

Your Wedding Planning Calendar
Four months before the wedding

	SUNDAY	MONDAY	TUESDAY
1			
2			
3			
4			
5			
6			
7			
8			
9			
10			
11			
12			
13			
14			
15			
16			
17			
18			
19			
20			
21			
22			
23			
24			
25			
26			
27			
28			
29			
30			
31			

Month

WEDNESDAY	THURSDAY	FRIDAY	SATURDAY

Your Wedding Planning Calendar
Three months before the wedding

	SUNDAY	MONDAY	TUESDAY
1			
2			
3			
4			
5			
6			
7			
8			
9			
10			
11			
12			
13			
14			
15			
16			
17			
18			
19			
20			
21			
22			
23			
24			
25			
26			
27			
28			
29			
30			
31			

Month

WEDNESDAY	THURSDAY	FRIDAY	SATURDAY

Your Wedding Planning Calendar
Two months before the wedding

	SUNDAY	MONDAY	TUESDAY
1			
2			
3			
4			
5			
6			
7			
8			
9			
10			
11			
12			
13			
14			
15			
16			
17			
18			
19			
20			
21			
22			
23			
24			
25			
26			
27			
28			
29			
30			
31			

Month

WEDNESDAY	THURSDAY	FRIDAY	SATURDAY

Your Wedding Planning Calendar
Month of the wedding

	SUNDAY	MONDAY	TUESDAY
1			
2			
3			
4			
5			
6			
7			
8			
9			
10			
11			
12			
13			
14			
15			
16			
17			
18			
19			
20			
21			
22			
23			
24			
25			
26			
27			
28			
29			
30			
31			

Month _____

WEDNESDAY	THURSDAY	FRIDAY	SATURDAY

Your Wedding Planning Calendar
Week of the wedding

1

2

3

4

5

6

7

8

9

10

11

12

13

14

15

16

17

18

19

20

21

22

23

24

25

26

27

28

29

30

31

SUNDAY

MONDAY

TUESDAY

WEDNESDAY

THURSDAY

FRIDAY

SATURDAY

NOTES

Chapter Two: The Budget

The budget will be a major factor in determining the number of guests you will invite, the location of your reception, the food you will serve, the number of photographs you will have taken, the flowers on display, and many other elements of the celebration.

Perhaps the best way to start is to determine what amount of money all of the parties involved—bride, groom, bride's parents, groom's parents—can and/or will contribute. As the section below outlines in detail, it is customary for the bride's family to bear the vast majority of the expense of the wedding and reception—yet circumstances can dictate other arrangements. For example, it is quite common today for the couple to bear all of the expense for the wedding celebration.

Regardless of who is paying for your wedding, you will need to know how much you have to spend and be willing to work to stay within those boundaries. Expect to make some compromises in order to stick to your budget. In doing so, you will be working to use your resources in the wisest possible way—to plan the wedding you want.

EXPENSES

Here are the traditional lines of responsibility for the various wedding expenses.

The bride and her family pay for . . .

> The groom's wedding ring and gift
>
> Invitations, reception cards, and announcements
>
> Housing for bridesmaids
>
> Gifts for bridesmaids
>
> Bride's wedding gown and accessories
>
> Fee for ceremony location
>
> Flowers for ceremony and reception
>
> Photography

Love is ever the beginning of knowledge, as fire is of light. — THOMAS CARLYLE

Music for ceremony and reception

Transportation

All reception costs (location rental, food, decorations, etc.)

The groom and his family pay for . . .

The bride's wedding rings and gift

Housing for ushers

Marriage license

Officiant's fee

Bride's bouquet

Bride's going-away corsage (optional)

Mothers' and grandmothers' corsages

Boutonnieres for groom's wedding party

Rehearsal dinner

Honeymoon

Two human loves make one divine. — ELIZABETH BARRETT BROWNING

Budgeting Your Wedding Worksheet

		Cost	Deposit	Date Due	Balance	Date Due
Stationer						
	Invitations	....	....	....	....	....
	Paper products	....	....	....	....	....
Guests						
	Accommodations	....	....	....	....	....
	Transportation	....	....	....	....	....
Business & Legal Matters						
	Marriage license	....	....	....	....	....
	Blood tests	....	....	....	....	....
Formal Wear						
	Bridal attire *(see page 88 for a detailed list of bridal attire items)*	....	....	....	....	....
	Groom's attire	....	....	....	....	....
Gifts						
	Gifts for bride's attendants	....	....	....	....	....
	Gifts for groom's attendants	....	....	....	....	....
	Gift for bride	....	....	....	....	....
	Gift for groom	....	....	....	....	....
Ceremony						
	Location fee	....	....	....	....	....
	Officiant's fee	....	....	....	....	....

	Cost	Deposit	Date Due	Balance	Date Due
Rehearsal dinner	....	....	....	....	....
Flowers					
Ceremony	....	....	....	....	....
Members of bridal party	....	....	....	....	....
Reception	....	....	....	....	....
Photography					
Pictures	....	....	....	....	....
Videotape	....	....	....	....	....
Music					
Ceremony	....	....	....	....	....
Reception	....	....	....	....	....
Reception					
Location fee	....	....	....	....	....
Caterer fee	....	....	....	....	....
Wedding cake	....	....	....	....	....
Decorations	....	....	....	....	....
Honeymoon	....	....	....	....	....
Additional expenses					
....	....	....	....	....	....
....	....	....	....	....	....
....	....	....	....	....	....
....	....	....	....	....	....

Family, Friends, & Finery

The

Dann

The

Kimb

Henry

Rob

This day I will marry
the one I laugh with,

Sa

Five

Saturday
C

Chapter Three: Invitations and the Guest List

You may be surprised at how important the stationer or printer turns out to be in the overall scheme of your wedding plan. Consider: You will probably order a good deal more than just wedding invitations. Depending on the formality of your wedding, you may also want to place orders for wedding favors, printed napkins, place cards, matchbooks, ceremony programs, or other paper goods.

Yet the most prominent part of your order is likely to be your invitations. It is this aspect of your wedding plan we will spend the most time with in this chapter.

CHOOSING THE STATIONER

If you have a friend or relative who can refer to you a reliable, affordable stationer, you are in luck. You can also find a stationer by looking in the local yellow pages under "Printers" or "Stationers." Bridal magazines often contain advertisements for printers, so ordering through the mail is an option—but be sure to obtain samples of the work and compare prices carefully before ordering.

Selecting your invitation

The invitation gives the first impression of the kind of wedding you will be having. Be sure that it reflects the style you want associated with your ceremony and your image as a couple. If the wedding is to be a simple affair, you will not want to purchase elaborate, embossed invitations—even if you can get a good price on them that week from your printer or stationer.

You should also keep in mind the weight of the invitations. Heavier paper grades of similar stocks will give a feeling of higher quality and have less "see-through."

By the same token, heavier stock, combined with a similar response card and the other necessary insertions, will require more postage than a lighter-weight stock selection.

Joy, gentle friends! Joy and fresh days of love accompany your hearts! — SHAKESPEARE

How many invitations should you order?

Once you determine the number of people you are inviting, you will need to place an order for more than that quantity of invitations. There are a variety of reasons for this.

It is true that you can expect a portion of the people you invite not to respond, despite your "R.S.V.P." notation. If only you knew who those people were ahead of time, you would not have to overwrite!

There is also a practical consideration: You will inevitably make a few errors in addressing the invitations, and will need new ones on which to place the correct wording. Finally, you should bear in mind that you will want to retain a few blank invitations as keepsakes.

What this all means is that you are best advised to place an invitation order for a quantity perhaps twenty-five percent above the actual number of guests you expect.

INVITATIONS: TEXT

Formal/traditional styles of invitations

1. When bride's parents sponsor the wedding:

> *Mr. and Mrs. Roger Parker*
> *request the honor of your presence*
> *at the marriage of their daughter*
> *Beth Elaine*
> *to*
> *Mr. Justin James Clark*
> *on Saturday, the fifth of August*
> *Nineteen hundred and ninety-two*
> *at two o'clock*
> *Center Street Baptist Church*
> *Fairview, Pennsylvania*

2. When both bride's and groom's parents sponsor the wedding:

Love knows no rule. — ST. JEROME

Mr. and Mrs. Roger Parker
and
Mr. and Mrs. Robert Clark
request the honor of your presence
at the marriage of their children
Miss Beth Elaine Parker
and
Mr. Justin James Clark
on Saturday, the fifth of August
Nineteen hundred and ninety-two
at two o'clock
Center Street Baptist Church
Fairview, Pennsylvania

OR

Mr. & Mrs. Roger Parker
request the honor of your presence
at the marriage of their daughter
Beth Elaine Parker
to
Justin James Clark
son of Mr. & Mrs. Robert Clark
Saturday, the fifth of August
at two o'clock
Center Street Baptist Church
Fairview, Pennsylvania

3. When the groom's parents sponsor the wedding:

Mr. and Mrs. Robert Clark
request the honor of your presence
at the marriage of
Miss Beth Elaine Parker
to their son
Mr. Justin James Clark
on Saturday, the fifth of August
Nineteen hundred and ninety-two
at two o'clock
Center Street Baptist Church
Fairview, Pennsylvania

Oh, what a heaven is love! — THOMAS DEKKER

4. When the bride and groom sponsor their own wedding:

The honor of your presence is requested
at the marriage of
Miss Beth Elaine Parker
and
Mr. Justin James Clark

OR

Miss Beth Elaine Parker
and
Mr. Justin James Clark
request the honor of your presence
at their marriage

5. When divorced parents sponsor the wedding:

Individual circumstances will vary. These are some general guidelines to follow:

a. When mother is sponsoring and is not remarried:

Mrs. James Parker
requests the honor of your presence
at the marriage of her daughter
Beth Elaine

b. When mother is sponsoring and has remarried:

Mrs. David C. Hayes
requests the honor of your presence
at the marriage of her daughter
Beth Elaine Parker

OR

Mr. and Mrs. David C. Hayes
request the honor of your presence
at the marriage of Mrs. Hayes' daughter
Beth Elaine Parker

Art is not necessary at all; all that is necessary to make this world a better
place is to love. — ISADORA DUNCAN

c. When father is sponsoring and is not remarried:

Mr. Roger Parker
requests the honor of your presence
at the marriage of his daughter
Beth Elaine

d. When father is sponsoring and has remarried:

Mr. and Mrs. Roger Parker
request the honor of your presence
at the marriage of Mr. Parker's daughter
Beth Elaine

6. Deceased Parents:

a. One parent is deceased and sponsor has not remarried:

Mr. Roger Parker
requests the honor of your presence
at the marriage of his daughter
Beth Elaine

b. One parent is deceased and sponsor has remarried:

Mr. and Mrs. Daniel Spencer
request the honor of your presence
at the marriage of her daughter
Beth Elaine

c. Both parents are deceased (a close friend or relative may sponsor):

Mr. and Mrs. Frederick Parker
request the honor of your presence
at the marriage of their granddaughter
Beth Elaine Parker

Love sought is good, but given unsought is better. — SHAKESPEARE

7. Religious Ceremonies

The following are general guidelines for those who wish to emphasize the religious aspect of marriage. If you have any questions, consult with your celebrant prior to making up the invitation with your stationer.

a. Protestant

Mr. and Mrs. Parker
are pleased to invite you
to join in a Christian celebration
of the marriage of their daughter
Beth Elaine Parker
to
Justin James Clark
on Saturday, the fifth of August
Nineteen hundred and ninety-two
at ten o'clock
St. Phillip's Methodist Church
Fairview, Pennsylvania

b. Catholic

Mr. and Mrs. Roger Parker
request the honor of your presence
at the Nuptial Mass
at which their daughter
Beth Elaine
and
Justin James Clark
will be united in the
Sacrament of Holy Matrimony
on Saturday, the fifth of August
at six o'clock
Saint Joseph's Catholic Church
Fairview, Pennsylvania

c. Jewish
(Approaches will vary by ceremony, and by Orthodox, Conservative, or Reform affiliation.)

To love for the sake of being loved is human, but to love for the
sake of loving is angelic. — DeLAMARTINE

8. Military Ceremonies

The rank determines the placement of names.

    a. Any title lower than sergeant should be omitted. The branch of
      service is included under that person's name.

Mr. and Mrs. Roger Parker
request the honor of your presence
at the marriage of their daughter
Beth Elaine
United States Army
to
Justin James Clark

    b. Junior officers' titles are placed below their names and are
      followed by their branch of service.

Mr. and Mrs. Roger Parker
request the honor of your presence
at the marriage of their daughter
Beth Elaine
to
Justin James Clark
First Lieutenant, United States Navy

    c. Titles are placed before names if the rank is higher than lieutenant.
      The branch of service is placed on the following line.

Mr. and Mrs. Roger Parker
request the honor of your presence
at the marriage of their daughter
Beth Elaine
to
Captain Justin James Clark
United States Navy

Less formal, more contemporary styles

Mr. & Mrs. Roger Parker
would like you to
join with their daughter
Beth Elaine
and
Justin James
in the celebration of their marriage

Love and you shall be loved. — EMERSON

Substitutions may be made where necessary. Your stationer can be helpful in resolving questions of etiquette.

ADDRESSING AND SENDING THE INVITATIONS

Your invitations should be mailed six to eight weeks prior to your wedding.

The process of addressing and sending your wedding invitations can be quite time-consuming. To reduce the potential for scheduling problems, some printers will provide the envelopes early to allow you to begin the addressing process right away.

It is standard to use black ink when addressing the invitations. Addresses are never typed. Another general rule is never to abbreviate names, addresses, or titles (with the exception of the words "Mr." and "Mrs.").

The writing on the outer envelope should incorporate the full formal name of the person(s) you are inviting. On the inner envelope, you may use shorter forms of the names accompanied by the names of family members (which should be listed under the parents' names). Following are two examples.

Outer envelope:

Mr. and Mrs. Lawrence Dean Jones
39 Elm Drive
Acorn, Michigan 45678

Inner envelope:

Mr. and Mrs. Jones
Justin and Shawn

Your return address should be written or printed on the outer envelopes; you will want to receive by return mail any invitations that cannot be delivered.

As discussed earlier, if someone you believe is planning on attending the wedding does not respond to an R.S.V.P., you will probably want to call. The failure to return the invitation may simply be an oversight.

"How do I assemble the invitations?"

1. Take the response card with its lettering facing up and place it under the flap of the response card envelope.

Love is all you need. — LENNON/McCARTNEY

2. Take the small piece of tissue paper and place it over the lettering on the invitation.

3. Place any extra enclosures (such as reception cards and direction maps) inside the invitation.

4. Place the response card and envelope inside the invitation with the lettering of the response card facing up. (Be sure to prestamp the response card envelope.)

5. Place the invitation inside the inner envelope with the front of the invitation facing the back flap of the envelope. (You want the recipients to receive their invitations with the lettering facing them.) Do not seal the inner envelope.

6. Place the inner envelope inside the outer envelope. The handwritten names of the guests on the inner envelope should be facing the back of the outer envelope.

7. Address and seal the outer envelope, making sure it contains both the address of the person to whom you are sending it and your return address.

8. Stamp the outer envelope and mail.

Note: The Postal Service usually has a line of "LOVE" stamps available in first-class denominations. These are ideal for your purpose, and will add a special touch to your invitations.

You may want to offer out-of-town guests a place to stay or make hotel reservations for them. Another considerate— and often essential—step is to include an attractive, legible set of directions to important locations with your invitations. (It is also a nice gesture to invite out-of-town guests to the rehearsal dinner.)

RECEPTION CARDS

Reception cards indicate where your reception is to be held. You will want to have these cards printed if your reception is being held at a different site than

Marriage is that relation between a man and woman in which the independence is equal, the dependence mutual, and the obligation reciprocal. — L.K. ANSPACHER

the ceremony. They are also important to include with certain invitations if your list of reception guests is not identical to your list of wedding guests.

Reception cards: text

Following are some examples of possible formats you can use in writing your reception cards.

Formal:

Mr. and Mrs. Roger Parker
request the pleasure of your company
Saturday, the fifth of August
at three o'clock
Fairview Country Club
1638 Eastview Lane
Brookdale, Illinois

Less formal:

Reception
immediately following the ceremony
Fairview Country Club
1638 Eastview Lane
Brookdale, Illinois

RESPONSE CARDS

Response cards are enclosed in the invitation for your convenience, of course; you need to know the number of people who will be attending your wedding or reception to better plan the proceedings. (The caterer, for instance, will need to know how many people will be eating.) The following are examples of possible wording for your response cards.

M _____
_____ *accepts*
_____ *regrets*
Saturday the fifth of August
Fairview Country Club

OR

The supreme happiness of life is the conviction of being loved for yourself, or more correctly, being loved in spite of yourself. — VICTOR HUGO

The favor of your reply is requested
by the twenty-second of July

M_____

_____ *will attend*

SPECIAL TOUCHES

The following items are products you can order from your printer that will lend a particularly elegant touch to your wedding.

Pew cards

Pew cards are used to invite family and friends to sit in reserved seating sections at your ceremony. They can be a good way to assure that those most special to you are seated closest during your ceremony.

The cards are usually mailed to your special guests after they have already notified you that they intend to be present at the wedding. These guests bring the pew cards with them to the ceremony, then hand them to the ushers before they are seated. Of course, if you go this route, you will need to place "RESERVED" signs in the appropriate seating areas before admitting guests.

Announcements

Wedding announcements are cards sent to those relatives and friends who are not invited to attend your wedding because of distance or other reasons. These cards are not mailed until the day of the wedding or as soon as possible after the date of the wedding. There is no obligation on the recipient's part to send a gift.

Thank-you notes

Thank-you notes can be ordered with the rest of your stationery. Ordering thank-you notes that match one's wedding invitations is a common practice, but you can also order more simple ones. If your alternative to specially printed thank-you notes is preprinted cards from a card or gift shop, you should bear in mind that it can be cheaper to work through your stationer. However, it is perfectly acceptable to send your handwritten note on your own personal (non-wedding) stationery.

Such is my love, to thee I so belong,
That for thy right myself will bear all wrong. — SHAKESPEARE

Stationer Worksheet

Stationer: _____

Address: _____

Phone: _____   Hours: _____

Appointment date & time: _____

Description of invitation (color, paper, type of lettering): _____

_____

Wording of invitation: _____

_____

_____

_____

_____

Description of reception card: _____

_____

Wording of reception card: _____

_____

_____

_____

Description of response card: _____

_____

Wording of response card: _____

_____

_____

_____

Paper Products Checklist

Product	Number	Price	Date & Amount of Deposit	Date & Amount Due	Total
Invitations/envelopes					
Reception cards					
Response cards/envelopes					
Place cards					
Thank you cards					
Announcements					
Pew cards					
Match books					
Napkins					
Wedding favors					
Book marks					
Ceremony programs					
Reception programs					
Groom's cake boxes					
Other					

Wedding Guest List

Name _____   Name _____

Address _____   Address _____

_____   _____

Telephone _____   Telephone _____

R.S.V.P. ☐   Number in Party _____   R.S.V.P. ☐   Number in Party _____

Name _____   Name _____

Address _____   Address _____

_____   _____

Telephone _____   Telephone _____

R.S.V.P. ☐   Number in Party _____   R.S.V.P. ☐   Number in Party _____

Name _____   Name _____

Address _____   Address _____

_____   _____

Telephone _____   Telephone _____

R.S.V.P. ☐   Number in Party _____   R.S.V.P. ☐   Number in Party _____

Name _____   Name _____

Address _____   Address _____

_____   _____

Telephone _____   Telephone _____

R.S.V.P. ☐   Number in Party _____   R.S.V.P. ☐   Number in Party _____

Name

Address

Telephone

R.S.V.P. ☐   Number in Party

Name

Address

Telephone

R.S.V.P. ☐   Number in Party

Name

Address

Telephone

R.S.V.P. ☐   Number in Party

Name

Address

Telephone

R.S.V.P. ☐   Number in Party

Name

Address

Telephone

R.S.V.P. ☐   Number in Party

Name

Address

Telephone

R.S.V.P. ☐   Number in Party

Name

Address

Telephone

R.S.V.P. ☐   Number in Party

Name

Address

Telephone

R.S.V.P. ☐   Number in Party

Name _____

Address _____

_____

Telephone _____

R.S.V.P. ☐   Number in Party _____

Name _____

Address _____

_____

Telephone _____

R.S.V.P. ☐   Number in Party _____

Name _____

Address _____

_____

Telephone _____

R.S.V.P. ☐   Number in Party _____

Name _____

Address _____

_____

Telephone _____

R.S.V.P. ☐   Number in Party _____

Name _____

Address _____

_____

Telephone _____

R.S.V.P. ☐   Number in Party _____

Name _____

Address _____

_____

Telephone _____

R.S.V.P. ☐   Number in Party _____

Name _____

Address _____

_____

Telephone _____

R.S.V.P. ☐   Number in Party _____

Name _____

Address _____

_____

Telephone _____

R.S.V.P. ☐   Number in Party _____

Name

Address

Telephone

R.S.V.P. ☐   Number in Party

Name

Address

Telephone

R.S.V.P. ☐   Number in Party

Name

Address

Telephone

R.S.V.P. ☐   Number in Party

Name

Address

Telephone

R.S.V.P. ☐   Number in Party

Name

Address

Telephone

R.S.V.P. ☐   Number in Party

Name

Address

Telephone

R.S.V.P. ☐   Number in Party

Name

Address

Telephone

R.S.V.P. ☐   Number in Party

Name

Address

Telephone

R.S.V.P. ☐   Number in Party

Name_____

Address_____

_____

Telephone_____

R.S.V.P. ☐   Number in Party _____

Name_____

Address_____

_____

Telephone_____

R.S.V.P. ☐   Number in Party _____

Name_____

Address_____

_____

Telephone_____

R.S.V.P. ☐   Number in Party _____

Name_____

Address_____

_____

Telephone_____

R.S.V.P. ☐   Number in Party _____

Name_____

Address_____

_____

Telephone_____

R.S.V.P. ☐   Number in Party _____

Name_____

Address_____

_____

Telephone_____

R.S.V.P. ☐   Number in Party _____

Name_____

Address_____

_____

Telephone_____

R.S.V.P. ☐   Number in Party _____

Name_____

Address_____

_____

Telephone_____

R.S.V.P. ☐   Number in Party _____

Name

Address

Telephone

R.S.V.P. ☐   Number in Party

Name

Address

Telephone

R.S.V.P. ☐   Number in Party

Name

Address

Telephone

R.S.V.P. ☐   Number in Party

Name

Address

Telephone

R.S.V.P. ☐   Number in Party

Name

Address

Telephone

R.S.V.P. ☐   Number in Party

Name

Address

Telephone

R.S.V.P. ☐   Number in Party

Name

Address

Telephone

R.S.V.P. ☐   Number in Party

Name

Address

Telephone

R.S.V.P. ☐   Number in Party

Name ....

Address ....

....

Telephone ....

R.S.V.P. ☐   Number in Party ....

Name ....

Address ....

....

Telephone ....

R.S.V.P. ☐   Number in Party ....

Name ....

Address ....

....

Telephone ....

R.S.V.P. ☐   Number in Party ....

Name ....

Address ....

....

Telephone ....

R.S.V.P. ☐   Number in Party ....

Name ....

Address ....

....

Telephone ....

R.S.V.P. ☐   Number in Party ....

Name ....

Address ....

....

Telephone ....

R.S.V.P. ☐   Number in Party ....

Name ....

Address ....

....

Telephone ....

R.S.V.P. ☐   Number in Party ....

Name ....

Address ....

....

Telephone ....

R.S.V.P. ☐   Number in Party ....

Name _____   Name _____

Address _____   Address _____

_____   _____

Telephone _____   Telephone _____

R.S.V.P. ☐   Number in Party _____   R.S.V.P. ☐   Number in Party _____

Name _____   Name _____

Address _____   Address _____

_____   _____

Telephone _____   Telephone _____

R.S.V.P. ☐   Number in Party _____   R.S.V.P. ☐   Number in Party _____

Name _____   Name _____

Address _____   Address _____

_____   _____

Telephone _____   Telephone _____

R.S.V.P. ☐   Number in Party _____   R.S.V.P. ☐   Number in Party _____

Name _____   Name _____

Address _____   Address _____

_____   _____

Telephone _____   Telephone _____

R.S.V.P. ☐   Number in Party _____   R.S.V.P. ☐   Number in Party _____

Name

Address

Telephone

R.S.V.P. ☐   Number in Party

Name

Address

Telephone

R.S.V.P. ☐   Number in Party

Name

Address

Telephone

R.S.V.P. ☐   Number in Party

Name

Address

Telephone

R.S.V.P. ☐   Number in Party

Name

Address

Telephone

R.S.V.P. ☐   Number in Party

Name

Address

Telephone

R.S.V.P. ☐   Number in Party

Name

Address

Telephone

R.S.V.P. ☐   Number in Party

Name

Address

Telephone

R.S.V.P. ☐   Number in Party

Name _____

Address _____

_____

Telephone _____

R.S.V.P. ☐   Number in Party _____

Name _____

Address _____

_____

Telephone _____

R.S.V.P. ☐   Number in Party _____

Name _____

Address _____

_____

Telephone _____

R.S.V.P. ☐   Number in Party _____

Name _____

Address _____

_____

Telephone _____

R.S.V.P. ☐   Number in Party _____

Name _____

Address _____

_____

Telephone _____

R.S.V.P. ☐   Number in Party _____

Name _____

Address _____

_____

Telephone _____

R.S.V.P. ☐   Number in Party _____

Name _____

Address _____

_____

Telephone _____

R.S.V.P. ☐   Number in Party _____

Name _____

Address _____

_____

Telephone _____

R.S.V.P. ☐   Number in Party _____

Name_____

Address_____

_____

Telephone_____

R.S.V.P. ☐   Number in Party _____

Name_____

Address_____

_____

Telephone_____

R.S.V.P. ☐   Number in Party _____

Name_____

Address_____

_____

Telephone_____

R.S.V.P. ☐   Number in Party _____

Name_____

Address_____

_____

Telephone_____

R.S.V.P. ☐   Number in Party _____

Name_____

Address_____

_____

Telephone_____

R.S.V.P. ☐   Number in Party _____

Name_____

Address_____

_____

Telephone_____

R.S.V.P. ☐   Number in Party _____

Name_____

Address_____

_____

Telephone_____

R.S.V.P. ☐   Number in Party _____

Name_____

Address_____

_____

Telephone_____

R.S.V.P. ☐   Number in Party _____

Name

Address

Telephone

R.S.V.P. ☐ Number in Party

Name

Address

Telephone

R.S.V.P. ☐ Number in Party

Name

Address

Telephone

R.S.V.P. ☐ Number in Party

Name

Address

Telephone

R.S.V.P. ☐ Number in Party

Name

Address

Telephone

R.S.V.P. ☐ Number in Party

Name

Address

Telephone

R.S.V.P. ☐ Number in Party

Name

Address

Telephone

R.S.V.P. ☐ Number in Party

Name

Address

Telephone

R.S.V.P. ☐ Number in Party

Name _____

Address _____

_____

Telephone _____

R.S.V.P. ☐   Number in Party _____

Name _____

Address _____

_____

Telephone _____

R.S.V.P. ☐   Number in Party _____

Name _____

Address _____

_____

Telephone _____

R.S.V.P. ☐   Number in Party _____

Name _____

Address _____

_____

Telephone _____

R.S.V.P. ☐   Number in Party _____

Name _____

Address _____

_____

Telephone _____

R.S.V.P. ☐   Number in Party _____

Name _____

Address _____

_____

Telephone _____

R.S.V.P. ☐   Number in Party _____

Name _____

Address _____

_____

Telephone _____

R.S.V.P. ☐   Number in Party _____

Name _____

Address _____

_____

Telephone _____

R.S.V.P. ☐   Number in Party _____

Chapter Four: Choosing Your Rings

Most wedding and engagement rings are made of gold, and it's not hard to understand why. The metal has an undeniable, almost mystical appeal to people the world over, and for many years it served as the standard by which currency was measured worldwide. The gold ring's unique role as a symbol of the permanent, binding nature of the wedding ceremony dates back for many centuries.

A word is in order on exactly how gold is classified. The carat system designates how many parts out of 24 are pure gold in a given piece of jewelry. Therefore, a wedding band that is "18-carat gold" is three-quarters pure. Gold wedding and engagement rings come in two varieties: "white" or "yellow" gold. The difference between the two has much more to do with personal taste than the value of the jewelry.

Since gold is such a soft metal, it is sometimes blended with another, stronger metal. While it may be tempting to choose "pure" gold, gold strengthened with another metal in this way is more durable. (This is why jewelry made of 18-carat gold is generally more wear-resistant than jewelry made of 24-carat gold.)

DIAMOND QUALITY

There are four categories for judging the quality of diamonds, known collectively as the "Four C's."

Clarity

The clarity of a diamond is measured by the number of its flaws or imperfections (either interior or exterior). Clarity, broadly speaking, is the most important factor in determining the beauty of a given stone: a stone with low clarity, for example, would have a number of imperfections when viewed under a gemologist's magnifying glass.

Cut

The cut of a diamond is the stone's physical configuration, the result of the

Love (is) the strongest and deepest element in all lives,
the harbinger of hope. — OLIVER GOLDSMITH

process whereby the rough gem is shaped. The diamonds you will be shown by a jeweler have had many cuts made on the surface of the stone to shape it and emphasize brilliance. The most common shape is the "round" (or "brilliant") cut, which incorporates a flat circular disk shape at the top of the gem, a modest, tapering edge around that disk descending to the gem's broadest point, and a sharper-angled taper to a point at the bottom. (Other common options include pear-shaped, oval, and marquise cuts.)

Color

The color of the diamond is also a major factor in determining a diamond's value. Stones that are colorless are considered to be perfect. The object, then, is to find a stone that is as close to colorless as possible—unless, of course, your personal preference dictates otherwise. (Many people prefer to wear stones with a slight discoloration, even though these stones are not worth as much as higher-quality diamonds.)

Many jewelry stores will use special blue lighting in their display cases. This lighting is meant to mask tints in the stone. Always ask to see the gem in normal daylight to get a better idea of the true color.

Carat

The diamond's carat weight is the final category. This refers to the actual size of the stone. (Unlike gold, the carat weight of a diamond is simply a physical measure of the weight of the item in question—and not a measure of quality or purity.) It is important to bear in mind that carat weight alone can be misleading. A three-quarter-carat-weight, colorless, flawless diamond will almost certainly be appraised higher than a two-carat-weight stone with several flaws and a murky, yellowish tint.

OTHER TYPES OF STONES

Of course, you don't have to have a diamond ring. Other precious gems like sapphires, rubies, emeralds, or amethysts can be quite beautiful. You may want to consider selecting your birthstone (see the following list).

The goal in marriage is not to think alike but to think together. — R.C. DODDS

January: Garnet
February: Amethyst
March: Aquamarine
April: Diamond
May: Emerald
June: Pearl
July: Ruby
August: Peridot
September: Sapphire
October: Opal
November: Topaz
December: Turquoise

Men's diamond wedding bands: an overview
The concept of a gift from an engaged woman to her intended, known as a return gift, has been a tradition for some time; equality between the sexes has only strengthened this ritual's popularity.

Many brides and grooms feel that the emotional significance of a diamond should be a shared experience, so more and more brides are choosing to "give the moment back" to their grooms by presenting them with diamond wedding bands.

Currently, 90% of married men receive wedding bands; of those, 20% are diamond wedding bands, a number that has been increasing steadily in recent years. The variety of designs of men's diamond wedding bands—and the fashion trends that have made men's jewelry as a whole more popular—are also contributing factors to the new prominence of the "return" diamond ring for men.

In Japan, the "love diamond" (as the return gift is called there) is usually a diamond tie-tac. Recent market research indicates that American men are somewhat more sentimental: they want to wear their "gift of love" every day, and on themselves rather than on an article of clothing.

Facts and figures:

    ❧ The average retail value of a man's diamond wedding band is $601.

For thy sweet love remember'd such wealth brings,
That then I scorn to change my state with kings. — SHAKESPEARE

    * The number of men's diamond wedding bands sold in the United States has doubled in the last ten years.

    * 74% of women expect to contribute to the purchase of their grooms' wedding band.

    * Recent surveys indicate that a majority of American men are positively predisposed to diamond wedding bands, both for emotional and fashion reasons.

Source: The Diamond Information Center.

THE RIGHT RING FOR YOU

The most traditional wedding ring is a simple gold band, although today there are a number of styles to choose from. Some brides choose to incorporate their engagement diamond with the wedding ring; others select an interweaving approach, with a wedding ring that "locks" onto or over the engagement ring.

    Although it is customary for couples to select matching rings, this is not a hard-and-fast rule. (Some grooms may prefer to go without a ring; for others, differences in religious practices may not require the use of a ring in a wedding ceremony.)

    However you approach the selection process, there are a few basic principles to keep in mind.

    * The ring should be proportional to the size of your hand. A bride with large hands may be able to wear a ring that, on another woman with small hands, would look quite gaudy.

    * Some jewelers are sensitive and considerate; others will, unfortunately, try to pressure you into a decision you aren't ready to make. When confronted with overaggressive salespeople, back off and say you have to think about the question overnight. It's your choice and your ring. You—not the salesperson—should be completely satisfied with your selection.

    * The diamond industry has spent a great deal of money in recent years to win broad public acceptance of the idea that two months of the future groom's salary is the "right" amount to spend for a diamond. It should come as no surprise that the industry is not necessarily looking out for your interests here. The "right" amount for you to spend on your ring is the amount you and/or your fiancé feel comfortable budgeting. There is little to be gained by spending what the diamond industry considers to be "right" on a ring if the effect on your finances as husband and wife will be distinctly "wrong" as you start your married life together.

Between Hope and Fear, Love makes her home. — RAMON LULLY

Choosing Your Ring: Worksheet

Bride

Jeweler name: _____

Address: _____

Phone: _____

Deposit/due date: _____ Size: _____

Notes: _____

_____

_____

_____

_____

_____

_____

Groom

Jeweler name: _____

Address: _____

Phone: _____

Deposit/due date: _____ Size: _____

Notes: _____

_____

_____

_____

_____

_____

Chapter Five: The Wedding Party

The members of your wedding party will have the honor of providing an essential support network for you and your fiancé, and will play a critical role in ensuring that all your plans come together on the big day.

LINES OF RESPONSIBILITY

The lists that follow will give you a good idea of the traditional roles and tasks undertaken by the various members of the wedding party.

You may choose to follow all of these guidelines; you may opt to observe only a few of them. Whatever approach you take, if you are careful to make all the lines of responsibility for the various tasks crystal-clear to everyone involved, you will go a long way toward minimizing the potential for confusion or error.

Weddings tend to go most smoothly when the members of the party know and understand the duties that have been assigned to them, and have the chance to review these responsibilities in detail at the rehearsal. (It is a good idea to write a schedule that outlines the duties of each participant and specifies the points in time at which each duty will be performed. You can circulate this "script" to the various parties whenever you feel it is appropriate to do so.)

Maid of honor

Helps bride with addressing envelopes, recording wedding gifts received, shopping, other important pre-wedding tasks

Arranges a bridal shower (with bridesmaids)

Pays for her own wedding attire

Helps bride arrange her train and veil at the altar

Holds the ring to be given to the groom until it is time to exchange it during the ceremony

Holds bride's bouquet while the bride exchanges rings with the groom

Signs wedding certificate (with the best man) as a witness of the wedding

Stands in the receiving line (optional)

Helps bride change clothes after the reception

Takes charge of the bridal gown after the wedding

Assists the bride in any additional planning

Love and fear exclude each other. — MACROBIUS

Bridesmaids

Purchase their own wedding attire

Help organize and run the bridal shower

Keep a gift record at the shower (usually one bridesmaid only)

Assist the maid of honor and the bride with pre-wedding shopping or other tasks

Help the bride dress for the ceremony (with maid of honor)

Stand in the receiving line (optional)

Best man

Organizes bachelor party / dinner (which is optional)

Purchases (or rents) his own formal wear

Drives groom to the ceremony

Holds the ring to be given to the bride until it is time to exchange it during the ceremony

Gives payment check to the officiant either just before or just after the ceremony (although the expense itself is customarily the responsibility of the groom and his family)

Disperses similar incidental checks to service providers as appropriate, by prearrangement with both families

Returns the groom's attire (if rented)

Ushers

Pay for (or rent) their own formal wear

Arrive at wedding location early to assist with setup

See to important finishing touches such as: lighting candles (if this is required); tying bows on reserved rows of seating

Escort guests to their seats according to family affiliation (*Note:* guests of the bride's family traditionally sit on the left-hand side; guests of the groom's family traditionally sit on the right-hand side.)

Meet, welcome, and seat preassigned guests of honor (such as grandparents)

Roll out aisle runner immediately before processional

Straighten up and clean after ceremony

Oversee transfer of all gifts to a secure location after reception

Help decorate newlyweds' car

Love is immortality. — PLATO

Mother of the bride

> Assists bride in choosing a gown and accessories, assembling a trousseau, and undertaking other important errands
> Assists bride in selecting bridesmaids' attire
> Coordinates her own attire with mother of the groom
> Occupies a place of honor at ceremony
> Is the last person seated before processional begins
> Stands at the beginning of the receiving line
> May act as hostess of the reception
> Occupies a seat of honor at the parents' table

Father of the bride

> Accompanies bride to ceremony
> Usually escorts bride in the processional, then sits with the mother of the bride
> Usually stays until the end of the reception to say farewell to guests

Flower girl

> Directly precedes bride in processional
> Wears appropriate formal dress (or a dress that matches the bridesmaids' attire)
> Carries a decorative basket filled with flower petals and tosses them along the aisle runner
> Is included with the bridesmaids in rehearsal, transportation, and photography arrangements

Note. Child attendants can certainly add a special charm to your ceremony. Just be sure the child you want to take part in the proceedings is not too young for the task. Children of about two years' age or younger are prone to bouts of sudden shyness or—even worse—violent temper tantrums. Children, like adults, will have their own personal reactions to public situations, and some will handle the assigned tasks better than others. The best advice is to select child attendants with an eye toward not only age, but overall temperament and maturity as well. Then include them in the rehearsal, work with them patiently, and appoint an adult who is good with children to watch and direct.

My bounty is as boundless as the sea,
My love as deep; the more I give to thee,
The more I have, for both are infinite. — SHAKESPEARE

OTHER SPECIAL PARTICIPANTS

No doubt there are a number of special people who are not members of your wedding party. Incorporating them in the ceremony can add a feeling of warmth and closeness.

Consider assigning close friends or family members tasks such as:

Reading scripture at the ceremony

Singing at the ceremony

Handing out ceremony programs

Circulating your guest book

Taking charge of the gift table and / or card box

There is something so indescribably sweet and satisfying in the knowledge that a husband or wife has forgiven the other freely, and from the heart. — HENRIK IBSEN

Wedding Party Worksheet

Bride's Attendants

Maid/matron of honor: ....

Phone: ....

Special duties: ....

....

....

....

....

Bridesmaids

Name: ....

Phone: ....

Special duties: ....

....

Name: ....

Phone: ....

Special duties: ....

....

Name: ....

Phone: ....

Special duties: ....

....

Name: ....

Phone: ....

Special duties: ....

....

Name: ....

Phone: ....

Special duties: ....

....

Name: ....

Phone: ....

Special duties: ....

....

Name:_____   Name:_____

Phone:_____   Phone:_____

Special duties:_____   Special duties:_____

_____   _____

Name:_____   Name:_____

Phone:_____   Phone:_____

Special duties:_____   Special duties:_____

_____   _____

Flower Girl

Name:_____

Phone:_____

Special duties:_____

_____

Groom's Attendants

Best man:_____

Phone:_____

Special duties:_____

_____

_____

Groomsmen

Name:_____   Name:_____

Phone:_____   Phone:_____

Special duties:_____   Special duties:_____

_____   _____

Name: _____   Name: _____

Phone: _____   Phone: _____

Special duties: _____   Special duties: _____

_____   _____

Name: _____   Name: _____

Phone: _____   Phone: _____

Special duties: _____   Special duties: _____

_____   _____

Name: _____   Name: _____

Phone: _____   Phone: _____

Special duties: _____   Special duties: _____

_____   _____

Name: _____   Name: _____

Phone: _____   Phone: _____

Special duties: _____   Special duties: _____

_____   _____

Ringbearer

Name: _____

Phone: _____

Special duties: _____

_____

_____

_____

_____

Chapter Six: The Gown and Accessories

CHOOSING YOUR GOWN

Some brides feel the gown they wear on their wedding day should be the most beautiful they've ever seen. Others have a hard time justifying extravagant expense for an article of clothing that will be worn only once. It's worth noting here that many of today's brides are opting to rent a gown, rather than buy one. However you approach the issue, you should make your selection with an eye toward the type of ceremony you are planning. If you have a large, expensive wedding in mind, for instance, you probably won't want to select a modest, informal gown.

The time of year you plan to marry should play a large role in your selection, as well. Heavy fabrics like satin, brocade, and silk taffeta are best for winter weddings. For a summer wedding, consider dotted Swiss, chiffon, or lace applique on lightweight taffeta.

The traditional pure white gown is no longer the automatic selection among today's brides. Ivory, cream, or other pale pastels are common—and perfectly acceptable—choices. Such alternate colors have become increasingly popular among fair-skinned women who may look pale and drawn in a pure white gown.

Should you wear white if you are getting married for the second time or more? The answer is a complicated one. Experts in wedding etiquette still feel that only a first-time bride should:

- wear pure white;
- wear a veil;
- wear a gown with a train; or
- wear orange blossoms.

How bound by these restrictions should you consider yourself? That will depend on the type of wedding you are planning and the people who will be attending it. Obviously, if you set great store by your family's reaction to such matters, and if they are likely to feel strongly about your use of "first-time" symbols, you should think twice before incorporating them into your ceremony. On the other hand, if those you are inviting to your wedding—family or

O, human love! thou spirit given
On Earth, of all we hope in Heaven! — EDGAR ALLEN POE

otherwise—are unlikely to notice or care about such issues, you can make your choices with a little more latitude.

<hr>

HOW TO CHOOSE?

The guidelines below will assist you in selecting the wedding gown that will best suit your wedding.

Informal wedding
> Formal, lacy suit or formal street-length gown
> Corsage or small bouquet
> No veil or train

Semi-formal wedding
> Chapel veil and modest bouquet (with floor-length gown)
> Shorter fingertip veil or wide-brimmed hat and small bouquet (with
>   tea-length or ballerina-length gown)

Formal daytime wedding
> Traditional floor-length gown
> Fingertip veil or hat
> Chapel or sweep train
> Gloves
> Medium-sized bouquet

Formal evening wedding
(Same as formal daytime except:)
> Longer veil
> Traditional floor-length gown

Very formal wedding
> Traditional floor-length gown (usually pure white or off-white) with
>   cathedral train or extended cathedral train
> Long sleeves or long arm-covering gloves
> Full-length veil
> Elaborate headpiece
> Cascade bouquet

<hr>

In the last analysis, love is only the reflection of a person's own worthiness from other persons. — EMERSON

THE BRIDAL SHOP

The operator of the bridal shop has seen it before. The bride-to-be bursts through the door, opens her purse, and passes over ten or twelve sheets of photos ripped directly from a bridal magazine. There is a problem, however: without the name of the manufacturer, there is no way to order the clothing! All too often, the original magazine has been discarded—and it is on another page of the publication that the necessary contact data was to be found.

Providing the right ordering information is only part of the necessary preparation when it comes to visiting the bridal shop. You should also decide approximately how much money you want to spend. Doing so will save time and make the selection process less difficult. (Why become entranced with something you know you will not be able to afford?)

It is generally a good idea to talk such issues over with a trusted friend or relative (typically the maid of honor or your mother) before you make the trip to the shop. This person should also accompany you on the visit itself to share in the fun, provide moral support, and offer insights on style. There will be lots of lovely gowns to look at, and it is very easy to be overwhelmed by the many choices if you go it alone—especially if it is your first visit to such a shop.

Allow salespeople to assist you in deciding which gowns are the most flattering on you. You may want to plan on visiting a few shops before making any commitment to purchase, both to compare prices and to try to locate the most knowledgeable salespeople.

When you finally choose your gown, be prepared to put down a deposit. This represents an obligation of sorts on your part— and on the shop's as well. Get a written contract that includes the boutique's cancellation policy; review this closely. The contract should also specify the delivery date of the gown, headpiece, veil, and all related items.

Of course, you should also keep a record of all your payments to the shop.

Fittings and alterations

Postponing the fitting until the last minute can cause unnecessary aggravation. Err on the side of caution! Arrange for fittings and alterations early, to allow extra time for any mistakes on the part of the manufacturer or the bridal shop.

Along the same lines, it is always advisable to call the shop to confirm your appointments for fittings a week or so beforehand.

Be sure to bring along your slip, other undergarments, and shoes to fittings; these are part of your attire on the wedding day, and modifications may be in order.

Accessories

You will need to accessorize your gown—not only with the veil, but also with other items such as jewelry. You will probably be able to buy or order the accessories at the shop where you purchase your gown. If you cannot, there are many specialty shops that will be able to help you find what you are looking for.

All accessories should be chosen with an eye to the way they complement your gown. The gown is the main focus—don't select any accessories that will overpower it.

Headpiece/veil

The headpiece and veil should match the style and formality of your gown. Ask the salesperson at the bridal shop to suggest good combinations—but reserve the final judgment for yourself.

Shoes and hosiery

Many brides break in their shoes before their weddings so they can be sure of being as comfortable as possible on the big day. That's one less thing to worry about! The hosiery you choose should accent the color of your gown. You may want to consider lighter lace or pattern hosiery in summer months.

Jewelry

The most popular choice is a single strand of pearls with modest pearl stud or drop earrings. Again, be sure your choices do not overpower your gown, but rather enhance it. "Overaggressive" jewelry selections can quickly sabotage an otherwise striking ensemble.

To fear love is to fear life. — BERTRAND RUSSELL

Slip/petticoat

Along with comfortable and figure-flattering undergarments, a slip will help the gown fit smoothly. A petticoat will puff out the skirt of your dress to add fullness and emphasize fabric details.

Garter

You are probably familiar with the tradition requiring the groom to remove the garter from the bride's leg and toss it over his shoulder to one of the single men in the group. (It generally occurs after the bride has tossed her bouquet to a single woman; each gesture is a playful attempt to predict the next person to be married.) The ritual can be fun; if you decide to incorporate it into your reception, you can order the garter from the bridal shop or from a variety of gift shops or mail order merchandisers. If you are at all uncomfortable with the practice, though, you will be perfectly justified in omitting it from the festivities.

Gloves

As noted above, it is customary in a very formal wedding for the bride to cover her arms entirely with long sleeves or long gloves extending over the elbows. Shorter gloves are appropriate for less formal weddings, with lace and net gloves two popular choices in this category.

Love keeps the cold out better than a cloak.
It serves for food and raiment. — HENRY WADSWORTH LONGFELLOW

Bridal Attire: Worksheet

Bridal shop name: _____

Address: _____

Phone: _____

Salesperson: _____

Hours: _____

Fittings:	Date	Time
_____	_____	_____
_____	_____	_____
_____	_____	_____
_____	_____	_____
_____	_____	_____
_____	_____	_____
_____	_____	_____
_____	_____	_____
_____	_____	_____
_____	_____	_____

Gown size: _____

Manufacturer: _____

Style and style number: _____

Color: _____

Delivery date: _____

Bridal Attire Checklist

	Cost	Deposit Due	Date	Balance Due	Date
Gown					
Alterations					
Headpiece					
Veil					
Shoes					
Gloves					
Hosiery					
Jewelry					
Undergarments					
Garter					
Other Accessories					

Chapter Seven: Wedding Party Attire

The attire for your wedding party should be coordinated with the style of your gown and your wedding's level of formality. All the elements must work together—or the overall effect of the appearance of the group may not be the favorable one you want. If you select an informal street-length style gown, you obviously will want to avoid selecting extravagant formal styles for your attendants—even if that is the style they have "always wanted to wear" as members of the wedding party.

CHOOSING YOUR WEDDING COLORS

One of the first steps in choosing your wedding attire is to pick your wedding colors. There are no hard-and-fast rules governing color selection, but there are some general guidelines to bear in mind.

> *In warmer months,* consider cool pastel shades, such as ice blue and pale pink.
> *In cooler months,* consider richer, warmer tones such as navy blue, plum, and burgundy.

SELECTING YOUR ATTENDANTS' DRESSES

You should start shopping for the attendants' dresses soon after you have chosen your own dress (assuming, of course, that you know by that point who will be in your bridal party). You may want to look through bridal magazines to get some idea of the styles you would like your attendants to wear. As you begin to identify the styles and colors you like, keep in mind that the final consideration should be whether or not a given item works well with your wedding dress. After all, that is the centerpiece of the occasion; you will not want attendants' gowns to be overly flamboyant in comparison with your dress.

WORKING WITH YOUR ATTENDANTS

Contact your attendants before you begin shopping; write down their dress and

Love is the emblem of eternity. — MADAME DE STAEL

shoe sizes, and try to identify any potential obstacles well ahead of time. You may want to ask your mother, your maid of honor, or one of your bridesmaids to help you in coordinating the many details here.

It is important, for instance, to consider the various figures, colorings, and budgets of your attendants as you evaluate potential styles. (The custom is for the attendants to pay for their own attire. One practical—and considerate—option is to select bridesmaids' dresses that can be worn again comfortably in situations other than a wedding.)

Note: In many formal weddings, the maid of honor is distinguished in a subtle way by wearing a slightly different style from that of the rest of the attendants.

Accessories

Like you, your bridesmaids will need accessories. Most attendants wear shoes that are dyed to match the color of their dresses; however, any shoe that complements the dress is appropriate. Another common accessory for attendants is the hairpiece. The best approach is similar to the one taken with dress selection: identical hairpieces that complement the bride's headpiece, but do not distract.

The flower girl

Your flower girl can wear any type of formal dress that matches or complements your wedding colors, including a dress in the same style the bridesmaids wear. Often, however, the dresses you select for the attendants will not be available in childrens' sizes. An all-white dress is a perfectly acceptable solution to this problem; one popular style is a lacy full-length dress with a sash that matches the color of the bridesmaids' gowns.

The bride's and groom's mothers

The principle here is a fairly simple one: Make sure these two women discuss their wedding attire beforehand so as to avoid selecting the same or uncomfortably similar attire! (The bride's mother traditionally contacts the groom's mother on this point.)

Where you go, I will go, and where you stay, I will stay. Your people shall be my people, and your God, my God. Where you die, I will die, and there I will be buried. —RUTH 1:16-17 (NEW ENGLISH BIBLE)

THE GROOM

You may think any suit or tuxedo will do, but there are certain guidelines for your fiancé to follow, as well.

The male attendants, the ringbearer, and the fathers of the bride and groom will follow the groom's style of dress. As with the selection of attire for the bridal party, you should consider the season and the time of day the wedding is to be held when selecting colors and styles.

Customary attire selections for the groom

Informal wedding

> Business suit
>
> White dress shirt and tie
>
> Black shoes and dark socks
>
> In winter, consider: darker colors
>
> In summer, consider: lighter colors or navy and white

Semi-formal wedding (daytime)

> In winter:
>
> > Dark formal suit jacket
> >
> > Dark trousers
> >
> > White dress shirt
> >
> > Cummerbund or vest
> >
> > Four-in-hand or bow tie
> >
> > Black shoes and dark socks
>
> In summer:
>
> > (Same as above, except:)
> >
> > Lighter color formal suit jacket

There is no remedy for love but to love more. — HENRY DAVID THOREAU

Semi-formal wedding (evening)

    Formal suit or dinner jacket with matching trousers (preferably black)

    Vest or cummerbund

    Black bow tie

    White shirt

    Cufflinks and studs

Formal wedding (daytime)

    Cutaway or stroller jacket in gray or black

    Waistcoat (usually gray)

    Striped trousers

    White high-collared (wing-collared) shirt

    Striped tie

    Studs and cufflinks

Formal wedding (evening)

    Black dinner jacket and trousers

    Black bow tie

    White tuxedo shirt

    Waistcoat

    Cummerbund or vest

    Cufflinks

Very formal wedding (daytime)

    Cutaway coat (black or gray)

    Wing-collared shirt

    Ascot

    Striped trousers

Love is not getting, but giving; It is goodness, and honor, and peace and pure living.
— HENRY VAN DYKE

Cufflinks

Gloves

Very formal wedding (evening)

Black tailcoat

Matching striped trousers trimmed with satin

White bow tie

White wing-collared shirt

White waistcoat

Patent leather shoes

Studs and cufflinks

Gloves

The Ringbearer

The ringbearer most often wears the same attire as the other male attendants. However, for a summer wedding, younger attendants can present a playful yet harmonious appearance in a tuxedo outfit with shorts.

Love produces a certain flowering of the whole personality which nothing else can achieve. — IVAN TURGENEV

Attire Worksheet

Bride's Attendants

Number of attendants: _____

Colors: _____

Style of dresses: _____

Manufacturer _____

Style number: _____

Cost per dress: _____

Place of purchase: _____

Address: _____

Salesperson: _____

Phone number: _____

Alteration fees: _____

Accessories: _____

Maid of honor

Name: _____

Phone number: _____

Fitting date: _____

Dress size: _____

Shoe size: _____

Bridesmaids

Name: _____

Phone number: _____

Fitting date _____

Dress size: _____

Shoe size: _____

Name: _____

Phone number: _____

Fitting date _____

Dress size: _____

Shoe size: _____

Name: _____

Phone number: _____

Fitting date _____

Dress size: _____

Shoe size: _____

(See pages 91-93 for information on selecting male attire)

Chapter Eight: Pre-wedding Parties

The engagement party; the bridal shower; the rehearsal dinner/party. Should you and your fiancé hold all of these? How should you plan for them? What about registering? These are some of the issues we'll be examining in this chapter.

THE ENGAGEMENT PARTY

Engagement parties are usually optional affairs seen by parents of the bride or groom as the time to celebrate your new commitment. These parties often represent the parents' first "real" opportunity to get to know your fiancé. It is common for the bride's parents to sponsor an engagement party, although they are occasionally held by the groom's parents.

Guests are usually limited to close friends and relatives. Many guests bring presents to engagement parties, but these are optional. If some of your guests do not bring gifts, you may want to consider opening engagement party gifts at a later time.

You may decide to withhold the announcement of your engagement until the apparently "conventional" party gets rolling—then spring the news to the group as a whole. That's a surprise people will remember for a long time to come!

THE BRIDAL SHOWER

Today's bridal shower is much different from the ones given for our mothers and grandmothers, in large measure because lifestyles today are different.

Many of today's brides have been living on their own or with their fiancé, and may not need gifts such as toasters, irons, or other "domestic" gifts. Joint gifts like cameras and compact discs are more common presents at many modern bridal showers. In addition, today's groom is often invited to the shower, once an exclusively female gathering.

Note. A "wedding shower" is one in which both the bride's and the groom's friends and family are invited. Even though the groom may be in attendance at a bridal shower, the focus is primarily on the bride, and the guests are primarily her family and friends.

Keep thy eyes wide open before marriage,
and half shut afterwards. — BENJAMIN FRANKLIN

The bridal registry

The bridal registry—which can be found at most major department stores—represents your opportunity to record your choices of patterns and color schemes for your home. Guests who plan to give you china, crystal, or linens, for example, can inquire at the registry before purchasing specific colors and patterns.

Registering can be a real convenience for both you and your guests. You don't have to worry about returning mismatched colors and patterns; they can feel confident they are purchasing an item you want. If you feel the practice is not for you, you may opt to inform your hostess of your preferred colors and patterns. The hostess can then include a brief note about your choices on the shower invitations.

Shower themes

Theme showers have become increasingly popular in recent years. These are parties with one overriding element that makes gift selection easier for the guests; the theme is specified on the invitation to the shower. The kitchen shower is appropriate for those brides who will be setting up house on their own for the first time; however, for those couples who have been living together, other themes—a barbecue shower, for instance—may represent a better "fit." In the barbecue shower example, each guest might give something having to do with a barbecue: a cookbook, a set of cooking tools, an outdoor radio, deck chairs, etcetera.

There are any number of variations on the theme shower idea; encourage your family and friends to be creative—and let them know if there are certain items that will be particularly welcome.

Showers: general guidelines

- The shower should be scheduled no closer than one week prior to the wedding. (Four to six weeks before the ceremony is the most common time frame.)

- *Always* invite shower guests to the wedding.

Love conquers all. — VIRGIL

- ❧ Provide your hostess with a guest list. (This is the only input you should anticipate having with regard to the shower.)

- ❧ Let your guests know that one gift per person is all that is necessary if you are planning a number of parties and want people to attend more than one shower.

- ❧ Send prompt and accurate thank-you notes. (Ask for help—perhaps from one of your bridesmaids—if necessary.) The note should include a description of each gift and the name of the giver.

Your keepsake rehearsal bouquet

You may want to save the ribbons and bows from shower gifts to create a keepsake rehearsal bouquet. This can be used at the rehearsal as a substitute for your real bouquet.

Gather all the ribbons and bows from your shower; stick the bows on a paper plate arranged in the form of a bouquet. Poke several holes in the paper plate and pull the ribbons through. Try to gather enough ribbons so that you will have a handful to hold securely.

THE BRIDESMAIDS' PARTY

This party (or luncheon) is the perfect opportunity to thank your bridesmaids and present each of them with a small gift. The gathering also represents a good time to coordinate issues such as transportation arrangements and other last-minute details. Traditionally, the bride hosts her bridesmaids' party on the day of the wedding, and invites her mother, the groom's mother, and any other close female guests. Sometimes the bridesmaids' party is the first real chance your guests will have to socialize together. It can be a welcome break from the hectic pace of the wedding week!

An alternative approach is to make the bridesmaids' party your "bachelorette" party—one last outing for you as a single woman. If you prefer this type of party, you may want to schedule it a few days before the wedding so you will all feel your best on the morning of the wedding!

An ounce of love is worth a pound of knowledge. — JOHN WESLEY

THE REHEARSAL DINNER

The rehearsal dinner is traditionally hosted by the groom's parents, although many of today's brides and grooms host the dinner themselves. The only hard-and-fast rule regarding the rehearsal dinner is that all participants in the ceremony should be invited. (This includes the officiant and any musical performers.)

There are three traditional toasts given at the dinner: the best man toasts the couple, the groom toasts his bride and her family, and the bride toasts the groom and his family.

(More detailed information on the rehearsal dinner is included in a later chapter of this book.)

Bridal Registry: Worksheet

Flatware

Formal:_____   Casual:_____

Pattern:_____   Pattern:_____

Manufacturer:_____   Manufacturer:_____

Dinnerwear

Formal:_____   Casual:_____

Pattern:_____   Pattern:_____

Manufacturer:_____   Manufacturer:_____

Serving Utensils

Formal:_____   Casual:_____

Pattern (if any):_____   Pattern (if any):_____

Manufacturer:_____   Manufacturer:_____

Linens

Bathroom colors:_____   Bedroom colors:_____

Pattern (if any):_____   Pattern (if any):_____

Manufacturer:_____   Manufacturer:_____

Other Items

Item:_____   Item:_____

Manufacturer:_____   Manufacturer:_____

Color:_____   Color:_____

Item:_____   Item:_____

Manufacturer:_____   Manufacturer:_____

Color:_____   Color:_____

Pre-wedding Party Gift Record

Party:

Date:

Gift Record

Guest	Gift	Description	Thank you sent?
			❏
			❏
			❏
			❏
			❏
			❏
			❏
			❏
			❏
			❏
			❏
			❏
			❏
			❏
			❏
			❏

Flowers, Music, & More

Chapter Nine: Flowers

Who can say why flowers are such an entrancing feature of the wedding celebration? Perhaps James McNeill Whistler came closest to capturing the essence of the flower as a symbol of love when he described it as "perfect in its bud as in its bloom, with no reason to explain its presence, no mission to fulfill."

It can be a mistake to take a hands-off attitude and "let the experts choose" when it comes to flowers. This approach can be particularly troublesome when dealing with reception halls, restaurants, and caterers who claim to "provide everything." The question is not whether such experts provide the flowers they like, but whether the flowers at your wedding will be the ones that complement themes and patterns you establish.

WORKING WITH THE FLORIST

The best rule of thumb to follow is to plan on ordering your flowers at least three months prior to your wedding.

However you approach selecting the florist, you will want to see samples of previous wedding arrangements. Note that photographs of arrangements can be misleading: the flowers you see in the photo may not even be available at the time of year you are planning to hold the wedding. (One of the primary jobs you will be asking the florist to do for you is to isolate the kinds of flowers you will be able to choose from at the time of your wedding.)

Plan on having a contract in writing with the florist. In it, you should finalize all pertinent dates and times, and the location(s) to which flowers will be delivered.

When you make appointments with your florist, be sure to bring along sample fabric from the bridesmaids', flower girl's, and bride's dresses. You will want to coordinate your selections against these shades.

If you are considering floral hairpieces for your bridesmaids and flower girl, your florist may be able to offer some ideas. Often, the florist will be able to provide arrangements that match dresses and bouquets—and may even be able to supply ribbon you can use to decorate the wedding cake knife, champagne glasses, and pews/chairs.

Be sure to ask whether your florist can provide an aisle runner, and if so,

There is a land of the living and a land of the dead and the only bridge is love, the only survival, the only meaning. — THORNTON WILDER

what kind. See it before you commit to it! Some of the cheaper runners stick to shoes, cause embarrassing amounts of noise, and move around too easily.

FLOWERS FOR THE CEREMONY

The flowers for the ceremony should not be overpowering; the idea is to allow them to create an attractive background without dominating the ceremony or reception. You can judge this by visiting the location at which the cermony will be held. Walk around: how would it look with the arrangement you are considering?

If your spot is a small, simple facility, you will not want tall, elaborate floral arrangements. By the same token, a more dramatic setting such as a cathedral will necessitate a bolder approach. (If you know someone who was married in the same facility you will be using, you have an advantage: find out what they used, how they felt about it, and whether that floral arrangement could work for you.)

Presentation

You will want to consult with your florist regarding the layout for the location of your ceremony and reception. After discussing the important features of the facility, you can move on to issues of presentation.

Following are some of the more popular choices with regard to ways to use flowers.

For the ceremony:
- Brass vases
- Candelabras decorated with ivy and ribbon
- Bows on chairs or pews (you can tie flowers into these)

For the reception:
- Old-fashioned wheelbarrow arrangement
- Around wedding cake itself
- Atop wedding cake table
- Atop buffet table

Only the complete person can love. —CONFUCIUS

   ᴥ   Atop wedding party table

   ᴥ   As centerpieces at guest tables (optional)

Hanging plants and small trees can also make for a nice reception decoration.

THROWING THE BOUQUET

This is a well known tradition; it is supposed to identify the next bride in your immediate circle of friends and family. The single woman who catches your bouquet after you throw it is, we are to conclude, the next in line!

The practice is completely optional; if you or your friends have any problems with this (or the associated ritual of the garter), feel free to omit it from your plans.

FLOWERS: NEW APPROACHES

Looking for something different? Many florists will be able to supply untraditional options that can have a striking and attractive effect.

For example, vine wreaths can be spray-painted white, then decorated with dried (or silk) flowers, white beads, and ribbon to create a beautiful piece for the bridesmaids to carry down the aisle. (These can also be formed into a heart-shaped wreath.)

Some brides have their bridesmaids carry fans that are elegantly decorated with flowers and ribbons; others select baskets filled with flowers as elegant carrying pieces. Each such carrying piece can also serve as a lovely keepsake for the bridesmaids.

Note: Many brides add some special touch or design element to the bouquet or carrying piece held by the maid of honor.

Special flowers

Another nice touch is to give each mother a bouquet of flowers (or a simple rose). This can be done during the ceremony itself or at the reception. Occasionally, ceremonies will incorporate a short reading expressing gratefulness to the parent(s) for the care and love shown through the years; the reading is concluded with the presentation of the flowers.

You may also want to order a bouquet of flowers to be sent to your parents

My beloved answered, he said to me: Rise up, my darling;
my fairest, come away. — SONG OF SONGS 2:10 (NEW ENGLISH BIBLE)

after you have left for your honeymoon. This is a welcome (and usually unexpected!) gesture of thanks to those who helped you the most in planning and carrying out your wedding.

MINIMIZING FLOWER COSTS

Flowers can be very expensive. If your budget is tight, however, this may be an area in which you can cut expenses. Here are some ideas for finding the right look for your wedding at a reasonable cost.

Do it yourself

If you, a friend, or any member of your family feel comfortable taking the endeavor on, you may want to consider this. There are a number of excellent books on floral arrangements; find one you like and consult it closely. Two words of warning are in order. First, give yourself plenty of time: not only must you come up with attractive designs well ahead of your deadlines, but you should also have the option of deciding things are not working out to your satisfaction—and calling in "the pros." Second, be sure you are just as demanding as you would be with the work of a professional.

Do it yourself—in places

Instead of using a florist for all of your flowers, you might choose to cut fresh flowers or wildflowers for certain key decorations. You can then ask the florist to focus on a narrower area than he or she normally would.

Use silk

Silk flowers are an increasingly popular alternative to fresh flowers. When they are done well, they can be quite attractive—without drawing notice to the fact that they are not "the real thing." Silk flowers can also be taken home and used as decorations or keepsakes. (There is another distinct advantage to using silk: you will have a much broader range of colors to choose from.)

He who has not loved has not lived. —ANONYMOUS

Move the flowers

It is a common practice to use the same flowers at the reception that you used at the ceremony. Simply place someone in charge of retrieving the flowers immediately after the ceremony and transferring them to the place where the reception will be held. (This person should be traveling, unloading, and arranging the flowers while you are having pictures taken at the ceremony site.)

When you are done with the flowers, you can give them to an honored guest or close family member. It would be a shame to let something so lovely go to waste!

HOW TO PRESERVE YOUR BRIDAL BOUQUET

The flower shop where you purchased the bouquet may be able to preserve the flowers for you, but this can be expensive. Many brides end up paying more to preserve the bouquet than they did for the bouquet itself!

If you decide not to have the flowers preserved commercially, there are a number of other methods you can consider trying on your own.

Pressing. This is one of the most popular methods. First, a picture of the bouquet is taken; you will need this for reconstruction purposes later on. Then the bouquet is taken apart, and the flowers are placed in heavy books between sheets of blank white paper. (This is to prevent ink from transferring to the petals.) The flowers are left in the book for two to six weeks, depending on flower size; a large lily will take longer to press than a daisy. Finally, the pressed and dried flowers are arranged in a design suggesting the original bouquet, glued onto a mounting board, and placed in a picture frame. For best results, begin this procedure as soon as possible after your reception.

Hanging/drying. The bouquet is taken apart and the flowers are hung upside down to dry. This prevents drooping and helps preserve shape. Most flowers will lose some color when dried, but you can minimize color loss by hanging the flowers in a dark place. When the flowers are completely dry (drying times will vary widely) they are sprayed with shellac or silica gel for protection. For best results, begin this procedure as soon as possible after your reception.

Potpourri. This method involves drying the bouquet and then gathering all the dried petals into sachets. To do this, cut some netting (or any lacy fabric) into four-inch squares and place a small pile of dried petals on each. Then tie the squares into small pouches with satin or lace ribbons. These sachets can be placed in your linen closets and drawers; the scent will serve as a sentimental reminder of your wedding day.

Love rules the gods as he will, and me as well. —SOPHOCLES

Floral Worksheet

Flowers for members of bridal party

Florist name:

Address:

Phone:

Deposit amount: Date deposit due:

Date of delivery: Time of delivery:

Location of bridal party:

Location of groom's party:

Date balance due:

Person	Description	Number	Cost
Bride			
a. Flowers			
b. Headpiece			
Maid of honor			
a. Flowers			
b. Headpiece			
Bridesmaids			
a. Flowers			
b. Headpiece			
Flower girl			
a. Flowers/basket			
b. Headpiece			

Person	Description	Number	Cost

Mothers of bride & groom

    a. Corsage

    b. Special
      thank-you flowers

*Grandmothers of
bride & groom*

Groom

Groomsmen/ushers

Ringbearer

    a. Pillow

    b. Boutonniere

Fathers of bride & groom

*Grandfathers of bride
& groom*

Musicians

    a. Corsage

    b. Boutonniere

Officials

Guestbook attendant

Other special helpers

Flowers for ceremony and reception

	Description	Number	Cost
Thank-you bouquets			
Aisle runner			
Ceremony:			
a. Altar flowers			
b. Pews/chair flowers			
c. Pew/chair ribbon			
d. Candles			
e. Decorative			
Reception flowers:			
a. Head table			
b. Cake table			
c. Buffet table			
d. Hanging flowers/trees			
e. Decorative			
Other			

Notes:

Chapter Ten: Wedding Music

Shakespeare said it best: "If music be the food of love, play on." The music you select for your ceremony and reception will mark the day in a special way—and will also serve to tell the world something about the way you see your love. Play on!

CEREMONY MUSIC

If your wedding is being held at a location where a musical director is a member of the staff, you can consult that person about questions you may have about your ceremony music.

Some places of worship will not allow your ceremony to incorporate "secular" musical pieces. These are musical selections that are not acknowledged to be religious in nature. Consult the officiant and/or the music director at your ceremony location to determine if there are any restrictions of this kind.

One good way to start your selection process is to find out what sheet music is available to the musician(s) who will be playing at your wedding. You can order additional sheet music if you need it, but you will want to know the "standard repertoire" you will be working with.

It is customary to pay organists and other musicians a fee for their services. Some places of worship will provide an organist for you; even in this case, however, you must plan on paying a fee.

SEQUENCE

Traditionally, the sequence for the ceremony music is as follows.

Prelude: Begins thirty minutes before the processional.

Soloist/Choir (if used): Begins after the prelude but before the processional—that is, immediately after the mother of the bride is seated. Of course, the mother of the bride is the final person to be seated before the entrance of the wedding party.

(If there is to be Communion, vocalists may also perform at that time. Vocalists

---

We loved with a love that was more than a love. —EDGAR ALLEN POE

and/or instrumentalists may perform at other points in the ceremony; talk to your officiant about where such interludes are to be incorporated.)

> *Processional:* Begins after the soloist or choir concludes, or, if there is no soloist or choir, immediately after the mother of the bride is seated.

> *Recessional:* Begins immediately after the bride and groom have been announced as husband and wife; continues as they and the wedding party exit.

(Make sure the musicians are instructed to continue playing as the guests leave the ceremony site. This will keep the atmosphere lively and pleasant.)

RECEPTION MUSIC

Your options for reception music will generally be broader than those for ceremony music. Among the many variables to consider are the age range of your guests, their musical tastes, and, of course, your own budget.

Live bands

Good bands are usually booked months in advance. There are many different kinds of bands to choose from. Jazz, classical, pop, or even a more eclectic style—the choice is yours. Your phone directory should provide a starting point for your search.

Schedule appointments to hear several bands play, or arrange to hear a demo tape of the band. (More and more bands are making these tapes available to couples looking for live wedding entertainment.) You will want to compare quality as well as price—no one wants her wedding celebration remembered primarily as "the time we heard that dreadful salsa group"!

After you decide which band is right for your celebration (and your budget), ask about technical considerations. What amplifiers will be used? How many outlets will be required? What kind of room will the band need? (It is possible, too, that you will have to rent some of the equipment if the band cannot provide it.)

Of course, some people are lucky enough to have close friends or relatives who are accomplished musicians and/or vocalists. If this describes your situation, your search may be considerably easier than the average. You should

---

Love comforteth like sunshine after rain. —SHAKESPEARE

remember, though, that it is customary to present such a close friend or relative with a special gift to show how much you appreciate the contribution to your ceremony and/or reception.

Specify exactly what type of attire is appropriate for the band to wear. Other important details you should confirm with band members include: the precise directions to the facility (write them down); the time at which they will be expected to arrive (early enough to set up equipment and be ready to play when guests arrive); your preferred musical selections; and the schedule of reception events.

(*Note:* You may want to ask the band leader to double as master of ceremonies in order to better coordinate the timing of special events such as the first dance and the cutting of the cake.)

Disc jockeys

Hiring a disc jockey is usually less expensive than hiring live musicians.

Disc jockeys can be real crowd pleasers, for a number of reasons. For one thing, there is usually a much wider range of musical styles available when working with a disc jockey. For instance, if your playlist includes both "Feelings" and "Helter Skelter," it's hard to imagine a live band doing a good rendition of both. A DJ, on the other hand, will meet the requirements nicely.

In addition, a disc jockey is generally seen as a less formal alternative than the typical reception band. If you are out to encourage a lighthearted, informal feeling at your reception party, a good disc jockey may be the choice for you.

Try to find a DJ who can appeal to the tastes of both younger and older guests. You will want to review the same points on attire, scheduling, and directions that you would with a live band.

Dancing

Group dancing begins after the traditional "first dances" (bride and groom, bride and father, and so on). To encourage your guests to become involved in the festivities, you should probably ask the band or DJ to play upbeat selections after these slower, traditional dances.

Love's mysteries in souls do grow,
But yet the body is his book. —JOHN DONNE

Suggestions for Wedding Music

Processional Music (Note: Choose majestic marches to announce the arrival of the bride)

Waltz of the Flowers	Tchaikovsky
Wedding March	Mendelssohn
Bridal Chorus (Here Comes the Bride)	Wagner
Trumpet Voluntary	Dupuis
Trumpet Voluntary	Clarke
Trumpet Tune	Purcell
The Dance of the Sugar Plum Fairies	Tchaikovsky
Ode to Joy	Beethoven
The March	Tchaikovsky
Ave Maria	Shubert

Ceremony Music

My Tribute	Crouch
The Lord's Prayer	Malotte
Panis Angelicus	Franck
Now Thank We All Our God	Bach
Saviour Like A Shepherd Lead Us	Bradbury
Cherish The Treasure	Mohr
We've Only Just Begun	Carpenters
The Unity Candle Song	Sullivan
Just You and I	Gayle & Rabbit
The Bride's Prayer	Good
The Wedding Blessing	Grieb
The Wedding Prayer	Dunlap
All I Ask of You	Norbet and Callahan
Wherever You Go	Callahan

Recessional Music

The Russian Dance	Tchaikovsky
Trumpet Tune	Stanley
Toccata Symphony V	Widor
All Creatures of Our God & King	Williams
Trumpet Fanfare (Rondeau)	Mouret

There is no disguise which can for long conceal love where it exists or simulate it where it does not. —FRANCOIS, DUC DE LA ROCHEFOUCALD

Pomp and Circumstance   Elgar
Praise, My Soul, the King of Heaven   Goss

Reception/Receiving Line Music
    Sunrise, Sunset   Harnick and Boch
    You Are the Sunshine of My Life   Wonder
    Just the Way You Are   Joel
    On the Wings of Love   Osborne
    Here and Now   Vandross
    Truly   Ritchie
    Hopelessly Devoted to You   Newton-John
    Endless Love   Ross & Richie
    Up Where We Belong   Cocker & Carnes
    Waiting for A Girl Like You   Foreigner
    The Wind Beneath My Wings   Midler
    Pretty Woman   Orbison
    Just Because   Baker
    Through the Eyes of Love   Sager/Hamlisch
    The Best of My Love   Eagles
    The Glory of Love   Cetera
    Always   Starpoint
    Could I Have this Dance   Murray
    Lady Love   Rawls
    Just the Two of Us   Washington
    Inspiration   Chicago
    Time in a Bottle   Croce
    Unforgettable   Cole
    Unchained Melody   Righteous Brothers
    Here, There & Everywhere   Beatles
    September Morn   Diamond
    Silly Love Songs   McCartney
    The Wedding Song   Stookey
    As Times Goes By   Berlin
    Woman   Lennon

Love begets love. —THEODORE ROETHKE

Music Worksheet

Name of band or company: _____

Address: _____

Phone number: _____

Manager: _____

Type of band: _____

Hours: _____ Cost: _____

Equipment provided: _____

_____

_____

_____

Equipment rented: _____

_____

_____

_____

Rental costs: _____

Notes: _____

_____

_____

_____

Selected Music for Ceremony

Before the ceremony: _____

Processional: _____

Soloist: _____

During the ceremony: ....

....

....

....

Recessional: ....

....

Selected Music for Reception

Entrance of newlyweds: ....

Music during the meal: ....

....

First dance: ....

Bride's dance with father: ....

Other dances: ....

....

....

....

....

Cutting the cake: ....

Throwing the bridal bouquet ....

Throwing the garter: ....

Newlyweds' last dance: ....

Other events: ....

....

....

Special requests and dedications

Chapter Eleven: Photography

If your photos are done well, they will bring you and your fiancé years of pleasurable reminiscing, and can serve as favored heirlooms in your family for a long time to come.

The common advice not to cut corners when it comes to selecting a photographer—even if you are on a budget—is sound. Of course you must work within predetermined limits when selecting the person who will photograph your wedding. But you should make every effort to choose your photographer on the basis of quality, and not merely on cost.

CHOOSING THE PHOTOGRAPHER

Start by asking family and friends if they know of a photographer with a good reputation in the field of wedding photography. (It's worth noting here that wedding photographs are a very demanding medium, requiring both stamina and quick thinking from the person behind the shutter. Someone who is known as a good photographer is not necessarily a good wedding photographer.)

If you have no luck on the personal-contact front, you can consult the yellow pages of your phone directory—or ask for referrals from people such as bridal shop managers or caterers who may already have established relations with photographers. However you come in contact with a photographer, bear in mind that the key to judging expertise is to see past work. Relying on verbal assurances of quality—even from "satisfied customers"—is not enough; what was more than adequate for someone else's wedding may not be at all what you had in mind. You should be ready to visit several photographers to compare their portfolios and prices.

Personality

In addition to considering the quality and cost of the finished product, you will want to take the photographer's personality into account. Most likely, you will want to work with a friendly, take-charge person who will be able to function easily and comfortably in a hectic atmosphere—and still deliver every shot as you request it. Tactful persistence, a cooperative nature, and organization are traits you will want to see.

It is impossible to repent of love. —MURIEL SPARK

Package deals

Inquire about package deals. These are sets of prearranged formats and quantities of photos that can often represent significant savings. A good package might include a number of 8" x 10" prints, proofs, parent albums, and your own wedding album. If you opt for this approach, you should check into the prices for additional pictures. For instance, how much will it cost you to have an additional 5" x 7" photo produced for a favorite relative?

WORKING WITH THE PHOTOGRAPHER

Once you have selected the photographer, you will want to schedule a meeting to discuss poses. You should also bring up any restrictions as to camera locations you want the photographer to observe.

Many couples ask the photographer to be as inconspicuous as possible during the ceremony; most are adamant about wanting to avoid flash pictures during this time. (Your church or officiant may have guidelines you must follow on this.) You may want to specify such details in your written contract with the photographer. Other points to confirm (preferably in writing) include:

- whether the photographer is to be present at the rehearsal;

- what time the photographer is to arrive at the ceremony;

- what arrangements will be made for the bridal portrait;

- what deposit amount is required and other issues regarding terms of payment; and

- terms of cancellation.

Your photographer and the wedding rehearsal

The question of the photographer's attendance at the rehearsal is an important one. You will probably want him or her to identify any obstacles or obstructions that will have to be dealt with as the ceremony progresses.

How much better is thy love than wine! —SONG OF SONGS 4:10 (RSV)

Making a picture list and planning the shots

A written checklist is essential. There should be no doubt whatever as to exactly what pictures you want the photographer to take at your wedding and reception.

One good approach to take here is to identify well ahead of time all the photos that can be taken prior to the ceremony itself. Taking these pictures before the fact not only streamlines the process, but also frees up your time considerably. (Why make your guests wait unnecessarily for you to show up at the reception?)

A good time for pre-wedding pictures would be two hours prior to the start of the ceremony. These can be taken at the bride's house (for the shots of bride's attendants) or the church. The photos of the groom's party are most often taken at the church.

Proofs

Once the proofs are returned to you, you will be asked to choose which pictures to print. Most people feel more comfortable consulting family and friends on these decisions. (Besides, doing so is a lot of fun!)

There are any number of reasons to consider purchasing photos for other than your own collection. Friends and relatives may want to purchase pictures for their own albums. You may decide to give each of your attendants a picture of the entire wedding party as a keepsake of the wedding day. Group photos can even make popular Christmas presents for relatives or members of the wedding party.

VIDEOTAPING

Many couples decide to videotape their wedding ceremony and reception. The great advantage of a videotaped record of the proceedings is that it offers a unique view, not just of a single moment, but of the entire experience as it unfolds—in both sound and image. The disadvantages, however, are worth taking into account as well. If a single wedding photo (or one of a number of albums) is lost or damaged, there are usually many others to browse through. If your videotape is lost or damaged, though, it is usually irreplaceable. And

Perdition catch my soul but I do love thee!
And when I love thee not, chaos is come again. —SHAKESPEARE

videos have been known to break (or be "eaten" by VCRs) after years of use. The best advice, then, is not to rely on the videotape as your sole means of recording the event, but to use this method in concert with your photography plans if you want a video record of the event. And be sure to make more than one copy of your wedding tape!

CHOOSING A VIDEOGRAPHER

Selecting a videographer is usually simpler than choosing a photographer. You may want to ask a friend or relative with the proper equipment to record the wedding for you; certainly, this is often an adequate approach. You will not be getting professional quality in this way, however, and you should be prepared to "fast-forward" through dull sections when you view the final product. There is also the sobering but undeniable possibility that your "draftee" may miss something important as a result of equipment failure or error.

The potential for such problems is minimized dramatically if you select a good professional videographer. Unfortunately, you will have to do some scrutinizing to be sure that the person you pay to do the job is in fact qualified to do it. The simple fact that someone possesses a video camera is no guarantee that the "professional" in question is any better than a relative would be!

As with a photographer, you should ask to see samples of past work on weddings. In addition, you should be sure to ascertain that the videographer can:

- edit the tape to highlight important sequences;

- isolate key moments identified beforehand;

- work within established positioning and lighting guidelines; and

- meet your budget.

Of course, it is just as advisable to compare quality of work and prices with a number of videographers as it is with photographers. If you are having difficulty finding videographers through personal contacts, you can always try the yellow pages of your phone directory.

Let us too surrender to love. —VIRGIL

WORKING WITH THE VIDEOGRAPHER

You will probably want to arrange for the videographer to tape both the ceremony and the reception. Attendance at the rehearsal is a good idea as well; there should be no doubt as to where people will be located or what the best camera angles are. As with the photographer, you may want to remind the videographer to be discreet with regard to lighting and positioning.

Consider arranging for the videographer to visit you and your fiancé separately before the ceremony. This way, you can each pass along a special message to your partner just prior to getting married—a message that will serve as a special (and probably very satisfying) surprise after all the dust settles.

Another good idea is to have the videographer briefly record the goings-on at the various guest tables at the reception. You will be able to use these sequences to remember all those who attended, even those you may not have spent time with.

Finally, you should be sure to arrange with the videographer to receive both the unedited and edited versions of the day's events. (However, as we have noted, you may have no choice here if you are not working with a professional.)

Love, all alike, no season knows, nor clime,
Nor hours, days, months, which are the rags of time. —JOHN DONNE

Picture List

Before the Ceremony

1. Bride and her attendants (getting ready)
2. Groom and his attendants (getting ready)
3. Individual poses of all attendants
4. Group photo of all female attendants and the flower girl
5. Group photo of all male attendants and the ringbearer
6. Groom and best man
7. Bride and maid of honor
8. Groom and his parents
9. Groom and his mother
10. Groom and his father
11. Bride and her parents
12. Bride and her father
13. Bride and her mother
14. Bride and her sisters and brothers
15. Groom and his sisters and brothers
16. Bride's grandparents
17. Groom's grandparents
18. Bride and her grandparents
19. Groom and his grandparents
20. Bride's parents with bride's grandparents
21. Groom's parents with groom's grandparents
22. Wedding book attendants

During the Ceremony (Processional, ceremony, and recessional)

1. Groom's grandmother being ushered down the aisle to be seated
2. Bride's grandmother being ushered down the aisle to be seated
3. Groom's mother being ushered down the aisle to be seated
4. Bride's mother being ushered down the aisle to be seated
5. Individual shots of bridesmaids walking down the aisle
6. Maid of honor walking down the aisle

7. Flower girl walking down the aisle

8. Ringbearer walking down the aisle

9. Father and bride walking down the aisle

10. Bride and groom exchanging vows

11. Bride and groom kissing

12. Any appropriate ceremony shots that do not require flash and can be taken discreetly

13. Bride and groom walking back up the aisle at the start of the processional

14. Bride and groom greeting family at the close of the recessional

After the Ceremony

1. Bride and groom together (several different poses)

2. Entire wedding party

3. Bride and groom with flower girl and ringbearer

4. Bride with flower girl

5. Groom with ringbearer

6. Bride and groom with maid of honor and best man

7. Bride and groom with groomsmen

8. Bride and groom with bridesmaids

9. Bride and groom with bride's parents

10. Bride and groom with groom's parents

11. Bride and groom with bride's grandparents

12. Bride and groom with groom's grandparents

13. Bride and groom with bride's immediate family

14. Bride and groom with groom's immediate family

15. Bride and groom with bride's extended family

16. Bride and groom with groom's extended family

17. Bride and groom with clergy/officiant(s)

18. Bride's and groom's hands (display of rings)

19. Bride's bouquet

20. Bride alone (closeup)

21. Bride alone (full-length)

22. Bride with bridesmaid's bouquets around the train of her dress (if applicable)
23. Groom alone (closeup)
24. Groom alone (full-length)
25. Receiving line (several different shots)
26. Bride and groom entering reception
27. The cake
28. Cutting the cake
29. Throwing the bouquet
30. Throwing the garter
31. Candids: guests at the reception (several different shots)
32. Best man's toast
33. Buffet table
34. Wedding party table
35. Bride and groom dancing together
36. Bride and her father dancing together
37. Groom and mother dancing together
38. Bride and groom getting into car
39. Bride and groom getting out of car
40. (Other special shots of your selection)

Photographer Worksheet

Photographer / agency:_____

Address:_____

Phone:_____   Hours can be reached:_____

Date & time needed:_____

Will attend rehearsal:_____   Date & time of rehearsal:_____

Deposit amount:_____   Date deposit paid:_____

Balance amount:_____   Date balance due:_____

Package includes:

❑   Proofs   ❑   8 x 10's

❑   5 x 7's   ❑   3½ x 5's (4 x 5's)

❑   Wedding album   ❑   Parents' albums

Date proofs will be ready:_____

Prices of additional pictures:

	11 x 14	$_____	8 x 10	$_____
	5 x 7	$_____	3½ x 5	$_____
	Wallet	$_____	Album	$_____

Additional arrangements:_____

_____

_____

Terms of cancellation:_____

_____

_____

Videographer Worksheet

Videographer:_____

Address:_____

Phone:_____   Hours can be reached:_____

Date & time needed:_____

Will attend rehearsal:_____   Date & time of rehearsal:_____

Deposit amount:_____   Date deposit paid:_____

Balance amount:_____   Date balance due:_____

Date tape will be ready:_____

Videotape will include:

❑   Pre-wedding preparations

❑   Interviews with bride & groom (individually prior to ceremony)

❑   Ceremony   ❑   Reception festivities

Package includes:

❑   Unedited version of wedding events   ❑   Edited version of wedding events

Price of additional copies of videotape:_____

Additional arrangements:_____

_____

_____

_____

Terms of cancellation:_____

_____

_____

Chapter Twelve: Transportation

What will it be? A long black limo or an antique roadster? How about an elegant Mercedes—or even that expertly reconditioned, gleaming '57 Chevy? When it comes to transportation, the options are almost endless. Let fun and your own sense of style carry the day.

Some brides opt for a stretch limousine, complete with stereo and bar; others take a more basic (and economical) approach and use their own or their family's cars. Of course, if you have access to a fancy antique car that is in good running condition (or know someone who does), you may want to consider that option.

In any event, you will need transportation to the ceremony, to the reception, and from the reception. So will your wedding party. If your reception and ceremony are held at the same location, your planning will be easier—and your costs will be lower.

Traditionally, the bride rides to the ceremony in one car with her father. Her mother and the maid or matron of honor ride in another car. The groom and best man usually occupy still another car, while the remaining attendants ride in a separate vehicle.

RENTING TRANSPORTATION

If you decide to rent a limousine, be sure to call several companies to compare rates. Most companies will require, well in advance of the wedding date, a minimum rental time (usually three to six hours) and a deposit. As with all professional services you hire, you should get a written contract that specifies the terms of the rental and the cancellation policy.

The driver should be given a list of the people he will be picking up, detailed breakdowns of all relevant locations, and the exact times at which pickups and dropoffs are to take place. *Important:* Well-written directions to your home (the driver's first stop) are a must!

The accepted rule of thumb is that the limousine should arrive fifteen minutes early. (Drivers are often asked to show up well before that "just to be on the safe side," but this entails extra cost.) Remember to tip the driver(s); fifteen percent of the total cost of the rental is customary. The best way to handle this is to place the tip money in an envelope (or envelopes), then ask your father or an attendant to pass along the money.

Doubt thou that the stars are fire; doubt that the sun doth move; Doubt truth to be a liar; but never doubt I love. —SHAKESPEARE

TRANSPORTATION FOR GUESTS

If you have guests flying in from out of town, most of them will need transportation. If you are part of a large family, you might want to ask some of your relatives to help in coordinating pickups and dropoffs. Some brides opt for a cab or limo service instead, but this represents an added expense and is usually not expected.

Parking at the reception may be limited; call ahead to reserve spaces in the facility's parking lot or parking garage.

Transportation Worksheet

Company name:_____

Phone:_____

Hours of rental:_____ Deposit/due date:_____

Total of transportation costs:_____

Transportation to the Ceremony

Passenger	Address	Pick-up time

Transportation to the Reception

Passenger	Location	Pick-up time

_____   _____ _____

_____   _____ _____

_____   _____ _____

_____   _____ _____

_____   _____ _____

_____   _____ _____

Transportation from the Reception

Passenger	Location	Pick-up time

Notes: _____

_____

_____

_____

_____

_____

Ceremony

Chapter Thirteen: Planning Your Ceremony

The ceremony will probably be the most special part of your entire wedding day. The format you choose will be determined in large measure by the religious traditions you and your fiancé are observing.

Of course, if your wedding does not incorporate a strong religious element, you will have a great deal of latitude when it comes to designing your ceremony. In this case, the only limitations are likely to be your own imagination and the cooperative input of your officiant.

Following are a number of suggestions/guidelines on ceremony sequence in a number of traditions.

THE PROTESTANT CEREMONY

Note: Protestant ceremonies can vary in content and sequence by denomination; the following list will give an idea of the common elements.

1. Music/entrance
2. Welcome from the couple
3. Prayer of blessing
4. Readings (often scripture)
5. Giving in marriage (Affirmation by parents)
6. Congregational responses
7. Exchange of vows
8. Exchange of rings
9. Celebration of the Lord's Supper
10. Lighting of the unity candle
11. Benediction
12. Recessional

---

*By the accident of fortune, a man may rule the world for a while—but by virtue of love he may rule the world forever. —*ANONYMOUS

THE ROMAN CATHOLIC NUPTIAL MASS

1. *Introductory rites*
   Entrance song
   Priest welcomes congregation
   Penitential rites
   Opening prayer

2. *Liturgy of the Word*
   First reading
   Responsorial psalm
   Second reading
   Alleluia
   Gospel reading
   Homily

3. *Rite of marriage*
   Declaration of consent
   Blessing and exchange of rings
   General intercessions:
   Prayers of the faithful
   Profession of faith

4. *Liturgy of the Eucharist*
   Offertory song
   Invitation to prayer
   Prayer over the gifts

5. *Eucharistic prayer*
   Introductory dialogue
   Preface of marriage
   "Holy, Holy, Holy"
   Eucharistic prayer

Even memory is not necessary for love. —THORNTON WILDER

6. *Communion rite*

> The Lord's Prayer
>
> Nuptial blessing
>
> Sign of peace
>
> Breaking of the bread
>
> Communion
>
> Communion antiphon
>
> Silence after Communion
>
> Prayer after Communion
>
> Blessing
>
> Dismissal

A Nuptial Mass is permitted if both partners are Catholic. The couple must also meet with a priest for Pre-Cana (pre-marriage) counseling to prepare themselves for responsibilities of marriage within the Catholic Church. Other preliminary arrangements (for instance, the posting of wedding banns) are required as well; plan on consulting closely with your priest at least six months prior to the wedding day.

THE EASTERN ORTHODOX CEREMONY

Eastern Orthodox (including both Greek and Russian Orthodox) ceremonies are similar to Roman Catholic ceremonies, but they feature a number of additional symbolic elements.

1. Wedding rings are blessed and then exchanged by the bride and groom three times. (Many Orthodox rituals are performed three times to symbolize the Holy Trinity.) The rings are then placed on the bride's and groom's right hands.

2. Crowns are placed on or above the bride's and groom's heads; these, too, are exchanged three times.

3. After a Gospel reading, the bride and groom share a cup of wine, each drinking three times. The congregation sings "God Grant Them Many Years," and the bride and groom walk hand-in-hand around the ceremonial table three times at the close of the ceremony.

Love is indeed a tender emotion, and you can make it blossom with a smile. —ANONYMOUS

(*Note:* There are a number of possible variations within the Orthodox ceremony. Consult with your officiant on the sequence you will follow in your wedding.)

Interfaith marriages are permitted only if both bride and groom are baptized Christians. Wedding banns are not required for an Orthodox ceremony, although they may be posted if the couple desires.

JEWISH CEREMONIES

Orthodox, Conservative, and Reform ceremonies share the following features, except as noted.

1. Rites are performed under a *chuppah* (an ornamented canopy). (This is optional in a Reform ceremony.)
2. The Seven Blessings are recited.
3. The bride and groom drink blessed wine; the groom smashes the glass (which is wrapped in a napkin).
4. The bride and groom are greeted with cries of *"Mazel tov!"* ("Good luck!")

(*Note:* Jewish weddings may not occur on the Sabbath or on any other day or time regarded as holy.)

Both Orthodox and Conservative ceremonies are performed in Hebrew or Aramaic only; neither branch will conduct interfaith ceremonies. Yarmulkes must be worn by men in Orthodox and Conservative ceremonies, and within these two branches the wedding band is placed onto the bride's right hand.

Reform ceremonies can differ from the Orthodox and Conservative weddings in several ways. For instance, the Reform ceremony is conducted in both Hebrew and English in English-speaking countries. In addition, the bride's wedding ring is placed upon her left hand in Reform ceremonies.

CIVIL CEREMONIES

The bride and groom are married by a judge or other qualified official in civil weddings.

A civil ceremony can be ideal for a couple looking for a small, simple, and inexpensive ceremony. (This type of ceremony can also be a good solution for partners who hold different sets of religious beliefs.)

Love is blind. —SHAKESPEARE

The stereotype of the civil ceremony is that it is held in a judge's chambers or in a courthouse. In reality, a civil ceremony can be just as elaborate as a religious wedding—and can be held in a home, outdoors, in a club, at a hotel, or in any number of venues. (*Note:* Many religious rituals can be performed at civil ceremonies as well.)

THE MILITARY CEREMONY

Military weddings are usually quite formal.

There are several unique characteristics of the military wedding that you should be aware of. First, of course, is the fact that the military bride or groom may wear his or her uniform. (The rest of the wedding party usually dresses in formal wedding attire.) If the military officer is the groom, he may wear a sword or saber, but never a boutonniere. If the groom does wear weapons, the bride stands on his right throughout the ceremony. (*Note:* Officials and high military officers are often reserved special seats at the ceremony.)

At the reception, military tradition dictates that guests be seated according to rank. It is also traditional for the bride and groom to cut their wedding cake with a saber or sword.

SUGGESTED SCRIPTURE READINGS FOR THE WEDDING CEREMONY

Your officiant will be able to help you select appropriate scripture readings for your ceremony. You might want to discuss any readings that are especially meaningful to you and convey the message you want to share with your loved ones. It is a good idea to consult with your religious counselor on scripture while you are completing your church's pre-marital program. Below are some suggested readings that are commonly chosen for marriage ceremonies.

Old Testament
   Genesis 1: 26-28, 31
   Genesis 2: 18-24
   Psalm 33
   Psalm 100
   Psalm 103
   Psalm 128: 1-4
   Jeremiah 31: 31-34

No cord nor cable can so forcibly draw, or hold so fast, as love can do with a twined thread. —ROBERT BURTON

    Ruth 1: 16-17
    Ecclesiastes 3: 1-8

New Testament
    Romans 8: 31-39
    Colossians 3: 12-17
    Ephesians 5: 2, 25-32
    Matthew 5: 1-12
    Matthew 22: 35-40
    Mark 10: 6-9
    John 2: 1-11
    John 15: 12-17
    1 John 4: 7-12

MAKING YOUR CEREMONY UNIQUE

There are a number of elements you can add to your ceremony to personalize it. Following are some suggestions.

Explain the significance of the unity candle, if you are using one. You may want to ask the person overseeing the ceremony to make a point of explaining the meaning of this symbol.

With your officiant, find appropriate places to update traditional wording. For instance, many couples today prefer the phrase "Who presents this bride?" rather than "Who gives this bride?" Another option: "Who blesses this union?" Be sure to discuss such concerns in detail with your officiant.

Use an unconventional vow, or write your own. Again, be sure to work closely with the officiant. (See the excerpt from Barbara Eklof's book *With These Words . . I Thee Wed* that follows.)

Incorporate new family reading sequences. It is interesting to note that the fathers of today's brides are being incorporated into the ceremony more than in years past. It is not uncommon now for the bride's father to write a short passage on behalf of his family expressing happiness for new couple-to-be.

Thank your parents. Your ceremony is a perfect opportunity to honor your parents publicly by asking a close family member to read a short of composition of your own. (You can even read this yourself if you feel comfortable doing so.)

Use trumpets! How about a fanfare instead of the typical organ processional and recessional? This can be a special touch that may fit into your budget more easily than you think.

Earth's the right place for love:
I don't know where it's likely to go better. —ROBERT FROST

Meet and greet. In place of, or in addition to, the standard receiving line, you can dismiss the guests from their seats yourselves. This means that, after the recessional, you return to the front of the building and, pew by pew, do what the ushers would normally do: Greet each guest and direct him or her toward the exit. This approach gives you a chance to say hello to people who do not plan on attending the reception or may skip the receiving line.

Make up a wedding program. This should include the schedule of your ceremony and the names of the bride, groom, bride's parents, groom's parents, all of the wedding attendants, and any other people you would like to thank or honor. At the back of the program you might thank your guests—and pass along your new address. (This can save you the step of printing up "at home" cards.)

Contemporary wedding vows

Two souls join today before witnesses, but we bring one heart only. I promise to work with you to build our love, to speak openly and honestly, to listen to you and maintain the respect and trust that's grown between us, and to love and cherish you—and only you—as my mate for all the days ahead.

ૐ ૐ ૐ

I (name), receive you (partner's name), as my (husband/wife). May we love one another with constancy, live joyously, laugh freely, and support our marriage through the trials and triumphs to come. As husband and wife, we will remember the delight that we have discovered in each other's company, accept the discoveries and treasures of growing older together, and provide strength where there is weakness. (Name), I stand before family and friends as your lifelong mate.

ૐ ૐ ૐ

Give all to love; obey thy heart. —EMERSON

I come to you pure of heart and sound of mind. From this day forward we will walk in peace, live by God's word, and trust in His blessings. If these include the joy of children, we will raise them in His sight and under His hand. I will always offer you support, friendship, and peace. I, (name), take you, (name), as my life partner, blessed in the certainly that where we take one step, God will take two.

From Barbara Eklof's *With These Words . . . I Thee Wed* (Bob Adams, Inc., $7.95). Used by permission; all rights reserved.

Hail wedded love, mysterious law, true source of humanity. —MILTON

Ceremony Worksheet

Location: _____

Address: _____

Officiant: _____

Date: _____ Time: _____

Location fee: _____ Officiant's fee: _____

Schedule of Ceremony

Opening words: _____

_____

_____

_____

_____

_____

_____

_____

Readings: _____

_____

_____

Prayers: _____

_____

_____

Marriage vows: _____

_____

_____

Music:

_____

Exchange of rings:

_____

_____

Closing words:

_____

_____

Additional notes:

_____

_____

Officiant Worksheet

Officiant/clergy:

Address:

Phone:

Meetings:	Date	Time

Fee:

Notes:

_____

Chapter Fourteen: The Rehearsal

When securing the location for your ceremony, you will want to insure that it is available not only on the day of the wedding, but also for a rehearsal prior to the wedding day. Since the ceremony rehearsal is the only practice everyone will have before the actual event, you will want to make sure that all involved know where and when the rehearsal will take place.

The rehearsal is usually held the evening before the wedding; however, if the facility is booked that evening, two nights before the wedding can be a workable schedule, as well. Regardless of when you must schedule it, be sure to hold the rehearsal! Skipping this step greatly increases the possibility of a serious error or oversight during the ceremony itself.

WHO SHOULD ATTEND THE REHEARSAL

In addition to the obvious choices (e.g., bridesmaids, ushers, officiant), you will want to invite other important participants such as musicians and vocalists. Sometimes the photographer and/or videographer are invited to review special instructions and any physical obstacles that will have to be worked around. You may want to invite close friends and relatives to share in the fun of the preparations (and add needed moral support). As noted earlier in this book, it is also a nice gesture to invite (both to the rehearsal and the dinner thereafter) out-of-town guests who have traveled a considerable distance to attend your wedding.

It is a good idea to send out written invitations to those you want to be at the rehearsal and dinner. This reminds everyone where they are to be and when, and leaves no doubt in anyone's mind about whether attendance is required. Sending out invitations is also a nice way to officially invite the spouses of members of your wedding party to your rehearsal dinner. (*Note.* Some of your guests are likely to need babysitters for the night; you can make everyone's life a lot easier by arranging for this, and letting parents know they can all drop their children off at a single, easy-to-reach location at no cost. If your budget can accommodate this, it is a very nice touch.)

Only a life lived for another is worthwhile. —ALBERT EINSTEIN

ORGANIZING THE REHEARSAL

Rehearsals can often be confusing experiences. (Better to be confused the night before, however, than on your wedding day.)

Consider designating a trusted family member—the bride's or groom's father, perhaps—to help "direct traffic." Of course, the officiant will be able to assist you in managing the section of the rehearsal dealing with his part of the ceremony. But there is usually a great deal that does not fall into that category—and must still be organized in sequence.

The order of the processional

Following is an example of a popular processional order. You may, of course, wish to alter it in conjunction with your officiant so that it is right for your ceremony.

1. The groom, best man, and officiants walk in from the side and stand at the front, facing the guests.
2. An usher escorts the grandmothers of the bride to their seats.
3. An usher escorts the grandmothers of the groom to their seats.
4. An usher escorts the mother of the groom to her seat.
5. An usher escorts the mother of the bride to her seat.
6. The ushers walk down the aisle in pairs (or escort the bridesmaids, or walk unaccompanied down a side aisle and stand at the front of the church, facing the guests).
7. (If bridesmaids have not accompanied ushers down the aisle) Bridesmaids walk down the aisle singly (or in pairs).
8. The maid of honor walks down the aisle.
9. The ringbearer and flower girl (the last attendants) walk down the aisle. (Although they may walk separately or together, the flower girl should follow the ringbearer if the two are not side-by-side.)
10. The bride and her father walk down the aisle.

The order of the recessional

The following is a sample recessional order. (All participants in the wedding exit down the center aisle.)

1. Bride and groom exit.
2. Flower girl and ring bearer exit.
3. Maid of honor and best man exit.
4. Bridesmaids, each accompanied by an usher, exit.
5. Bride's parents exit.
6. Groom's parents exit.
7. Bride's grandparents exit.
8. Groom's grandparents exit.

Note: The bride's and groom's parents sometimes exit directly after the bride and groom, followed by the rest of the wedding party. The order of both the processional and the recessional may vary by tradition or denomination. Consult with your officiant.

Final details

Writing and circulating a list of assigned responsibilities prior to the rehearsal will bring a measure of order to the proceedings. This list should include not only the given person's duties or position, but also when key tasks are to be performed. (For instance, "John Smith will light the candles at the side of the church at 4:45 p.m.")

If everyone has a schedule, and if you designate someone to help take charge of the rehearsal, things should flow relatively smoothly. Remember that now (rather than the wedding) is the time for questions and mistakes—so try not to be too nervous if the evening is less than perfect.

Love consists in this, that two solitudes protect and touch and greet each other.
—RAINER MARIA RILKE

The ushers

Following is a list of some of the most common duties that will need to be delegated among your ushers.

1. *Seat the guests.* Be sure those who are seating the guests know that the bride's guests are seated on the left (as the usher is facing the altar), and the groom's guests are seated on the right. Ushers must be prepared to ask guests whether they are a friend of the bride or the groom, and must know which seats are reserved and for whom. Ushers should also be prepared to assign seats in such a way as to avoid an "uneven" look. (This may entail seating guests of the groom on the bride's side, or vice-versa, although a look at your guest list should help you determine whether there will be a problem on this score.)

2. *Roll out the aisle runner.* Assign two ushers to this task.

3. *Light candles.* (If this is applicable to your wedding.)

4. *Seat honored guests in prearranged spots.* Specific ushers should be on the lookout for specific members of the wedding families (grandmother of the groom, grandmother of the bride, mother of the groom, mother of the bride) as the ceremony requires, and to seat them in the proper spots.

THE REHEARSAL DINNER

The rehearsal dinner, usually held immediately after the rehearsal itself, can be as simple as a barbecue in the backyard or as formal as a seven-course dinner in the ballroom of a grand hotel. Of course, if you plan on a more formal approach you will want to make your plans well in advance. You should invite all those who took part in the rehearsal, including the officiant.

If you feel it is appropriate and will make your guests more comfortable, establish a seating arrangement that allows those who know each other to sit together. At some point during the dinner, you and your fiancé should make a point of thanking all those who have played a part in helping you organize the wedding up to this point.

Important: At evening's end, before the group disperses, be sure that everyone is aware of exactly when it is necessary to meet at the wedding location.

I wonder by my troth, what thou and I did till we lov'd? —JOHN DONNE

Rehearsal Dinner Worksheet

Rehearsal location: _____

Contact: _____

Phone: _____ Hours: _____

Appointments

Date: _____ Time: _____

Date: _____ Time: _____

Date: _____ Time: _____

Menu: _____

_____

_____

_____

Rehearsal location: _____

Contact: _____

Phone: _____ Hours: _____

Appointments

Date: _____ Time: _____

Date: _____ Time: _____

Date: _____ Time: _____

Menu: _____

_____

_____

_____

Seating Plan Grid for Rehearsal Dinner

Reception

Chapter Fifteen: The Reception Facility and the Caterer

Your reception should be a joyous occasion—the party you'll remember for a lifetime. Of course, a lot of careful planning will go into that celebration. In previous chapters, we've examined many of the issues associated with organizing services such as music and flowers for your reception. There are still a number of issues to be examined on the matter of planning the party itself, and that is the focus of this section of the book.

LOCATION

There are any number of options available to you, and your only real limits will be your budget and the size of the party you have in mind—and time, of course. You will want to settle on your location early; many halls, restaurants, and hotels are booked up to a year in advance.

Some possibilities for your reception location follow.

- Restaurant

- Hotel

- Fraternal society function hall

- Outdoor location (for instance, a lakeside reception)

- Family home (especially effective in a large historic house)

In the end, the possibilities fall into two main categories: you will either be in a facility that does not offer food service, or in one that does.

Note: Once you do select your reception facility, you will want, as with your other arrangements, to obtain a written contract specifying all relevant dates, times, and obligations; you should also be prepared to put down a deposit.

SELECTING THE CATERER

If there is no food service provided at the site you select, you will probably want

Love and attraction between men and women . . . is the very finest relationship.
—MARGARET SANGER

to think about hiring a caterer. (If you have a gourmet cook in your family who does not mind serving a large party, you may be the lucky exception to this.) A service referred by family or friends is usually a safe choice, but be sure to shop around and compare prices even if you do have such a lead; there may be some negotiating room. Always ask to see photographs of past receptions the caterer has supplied.

Be sure your contract with the caterer includes all relevant dates, costs, and cancellation clauses. Here, too, you will probably be asked to put down a deposit. Most caterers require this before they will reserve the date and time you specify.

Of course, by the time you make your arrangements with the caterer, you will need to know not only where the reception will be held, but how many people will be attending.

Ironing out the details with your caterer

Following are a number of issues you will want to address with your caterer.

- Does the caterer provide linens? What about flatware?

- Are waiters/waitresses included in your agreement?

- Will decorations be provided for the food? If so, will they match your established themes?

- Can the caterer provide the wedding cake? If so, who will serve the cake to the guests? (You may opt to have the bridesmaids handle this task; it will give them a chance to mingle with family and friends.)

- Are taxes and gratuities included in the price?

SIT-DOWN vs. BUFFET

The sit-down or the buffet: which is right for you?

The sit-down meal is usually considered to be the more formal option—but don't rule out the buffet-style approach immediately. A buffet can carry its own unique elegance, and can contribute to a livelier level of conversation among your guests. Bear in mind, too, that the sit-down meal is generally more expensive than the buffet: it almost always requires waiters and

That Love is all there is,
Is all we know of Love . . . —EMILY DICKINSON

waitresses to serve the (hot) selections. The buffet, by contrast, can include cold foods exclusively, cold foods and hot selections side-by-side, or all hot menu items.

THE MENU

The first consideration here is a simple one. What time of day will the reception be held? If your guests have been sitting at the church since eleven-thirty, you will not want to offer them a sparse selection of hors d'oeuvres and soft drinks when they arrive at your reception at one o'clock. Lunch is in order!

If you are trying to cut costs, you may opt to have your wedding and reception scheduled in between main meal times. "Snacking" foods are appropriate in such a time slot.

For detailed ideas on your menu, see the following tables.

Menu Suggestions

Hors d'oeuvres

Barbecued Chicken Wings	Beef Teriyaki
Chicken Fingers	Chicken Wings
Clams	Clam Cakes
Crab Cakes	Crab Legs
Crabmeat	Fried Mushrooms
Italian Sausages	Lobster
Meat Balls	Mozzarella Sticks
Oysters	Pork Loin with Sweet & Sour
Potato Skins with Cheese Sauce	Quiche Lorraine
Roasted Mussels	Scallops
Shrimp Cocktail	Shrimp Scampi
Smoked Salmon	Spring Rolls

Luncheon or Dinner Entrees

Baked Scrod	Baked Stuffed Shrimp
Boiled or Baked Ham	Boneless Breast of Chicken
Breast of Capon	Chicken Cordon Bleu
Filet of Scrod	Filet of Sole

Love is enough, though the world be a-waning. —WILLIAM MORRIS

Filet Mignon   Grilled or Poached Salmon
Grilled Swordfish   Pheasant
Prime Rib   Roast Beef
Seafood Newburg   Sirloin Steak
Veal Steak

Salads

Caesar Salad   Chef Salad
Chicken Salad   Coleslaw
Garden Tossed Salad   Greek Salad
Jello Salad   Lobster Salad
Macaroni Salad   Pasta Salad
Potato Salad   Spinach Salad
Tuna Salad

Soups

Fish Chowder   French Onion Soup
Hot & Sour Soup   Minestrone Soup
Mushroom Soup   Oyster Stew
New England Clam Chowder   Vegetable Soup

Buffet Entres

Baked Ham   Chicken Cordon Bleu
Chicken Kiev   Fried Chicken
Hot or Cold Ham   Hot or Cold Roast Beef
Hot or Cold Turkey Breast   Roast Beef
Stuffed Chicken   Swedish Meatballs
Ziti with Meatballs

Desserts

Apple Strudel   Boston Cream Pie
Cheesecake   Cherries Jubilee
Chocolate Mint Pie   Chocolate Mousse
Fresh Fruit Cup   Ice Cream
Sherbet   Strawberry Shortcake

Cheeses

Longhorn   Muenster
Swiss   White American

Snacks
> Crackers
> Peanuts/Mixed Nuts
> Pretzels

Drinks
> *Hot*
> Coffee
> Tea
>
> *Cold*
> Juices
> Milk
> Mineral Water
> Punch
> Soft Drinks

Wines
> *Red*
> Bardolino, Bolla
> Beaujolias Village, George Du Boeuf
> Cabernet Sauvignon, Buena Vista
> Chateauneuf-du-Pape, Chateau Mont-Redon
>
> *White*
> Chablis, Bouchard-Pere & Fils
> Chardonnay, Robert Mondavi
> Chardonnay, Dry Creek
> Pouilly Fuisse, Louis Jadot
>
> *Blush*
> White Grenache, Gallo
> White Zinfandel, Robert Mondavi
> White Zinfandel, Sebastiani
>
> *Champagne*
> Brut, Freixenet
> Brut Rose, Korbel
> White Star, Moet et Chandon

Reception Worksheet

Reception location:

Contact person:

Address:

Phone: Hours:

Date & amount of deposit: Date & amount of balance:

Total amount due: Date & time of rental:

Reception location includes:

Terms of cancellation:

Caterer Worksheet

Address:_____

Phone:_____ Hours:_____

Appointments:

Date:_____ Time:_____

Date:_____ Time:_____

Date:_____ Time:_____

Date & time of hired services:_____

_____

Menu:_____

_____

_____

_____

Includes the following services and equipment:_____

_____

_____

_____

_____

Terms of cancellation:_____

_____

_____

_____

Planning Your Menu Worksheet

Sit-down or buffet? _____

Food: _____

_____

_____

_____

_____

_____

_____

Desserts: _____

_____

_____

Drinks (punch, coffee, tea, liquor) _____

_____

_____

Snacks (mints, peanuts, etc.): _____

_____

_____

Other: _____

_____

_____

_____

_____

Caterer Expense Worksheet

	Cost
Food	....
Beverages	....
Linens	....
Flatware	....
Plates	....
Serving pieces	....
Rental equipment	....
Waiters/bartenders	....
Gratuities	....
Other	....
....	....
....	....
....	....
....	....
....	....
....	....
....	....
....	....

Total: ....

Seating Plan Grid for Reception

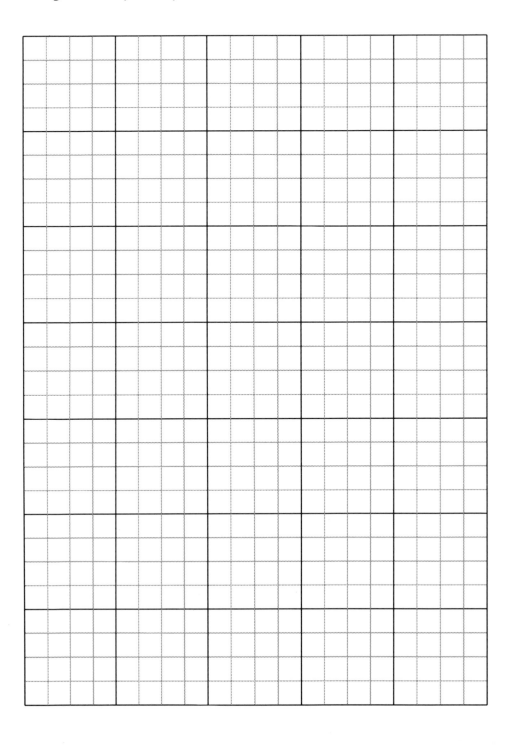

Chapter Sixteen: Your Wedding Cake

How inventive can you be in designing a customized wedding cake? We know of one couple who took their shared adoration of the Rocky and Bullwinkle cartoon series and made it the theme, not only of their cake, but of the whole reception!

Most couples have tastes that are somewhat more subdued. Even if you do not have an urge to experiment with wild themes, you can still find the wedding cake that expresses your own personal sense of style. Some caterers, hotels, or restaurants can provide a suitable wedding cake along with the food service offered. If you do have to find a baker, however, you will not want to put off doing so until the last minute. Wedding cakes must usually be ordered at least one to two months prior to the wedding day.

WORKING WITH THE BAKER

The price of your cake will be based on the number of people you have to serve—and on the kind of cake you have in mind. Comparison shopping here, as elsewhere, is highly recommended. You may be able to save a great deal, without compromises on quality, by speaking to several bakers before making any commitments. (Ask to see photos of the baker's previous work.) There is also the advantage that by following this method you will be able to "sample the goods" via a personal taste test at a number of different bakeries!

If you have seen magazine pictures of wedding cakes you like, clip them out and bring them to your meetings. Often, this will be enough for the baker to go on to give you a "ballpark" cost estimate on the spot.

Flavors, fillings, and toppings

Traditional flavors for wedding cakes include chocolate, "white," and "yellow." More and more of today's couples, however, are opting for less conventional flavor selections. Here are some of the possibilities.

- Cheesecake

- German chocolate

Love is most nearly itself
When here and now cease to matter. —T.S. ELIOT

- ❧ Fruit liqueur

- ❧ Carrot

- ❧ Banana

- ❧ Mocha

Many wedding cakes also include some variety of filling. There are a number of delicious alternatives, including lemon, custard, raspberry, and mocha. As for toppings, most cakes incorporate some kind of butter cream icing or whipped cream.

Let your imagination run wild—then think about your selection overnight before placing the order. You may realize that an extremely esoteric selection will not sit well with all of your guests.

Shapes and sizes

The conventional shapes—round, square, rectangular, heart-shaped—are certainly safe choices. Most of today's bakers, however, are capable of making your cake in virtually any shape. If there is a special design or motif you want to emphasize with your cake, you have nothing to lose by asking for pricing.

If you have a very large number of guests, one cake may not be enough. The best solution is to order a number of sheet cakes to accompany the main cake.

Decorations

These can be as elaborate or as simple as your reception atmosphere dictates.

Looking at pictures of the various cakes in wedding magazines or the photos your baker supplies will help you decide what icing and decoration styles you like best. If you decide to incorporate a cake top with figurines, you may be able to order these through the baker. Alternative ideas for cake tops include floral arrangements, silk flowers, or even mementos of an important shared interest or experience.

True love is rooted in a recognition of the beloved's moral and mental identity.
—BARON RICHARD VON KRAFFT-EBING

THE GROOM'S CAKE

This is a rich fruit cake traditionally given out piece-by-piece, in boxes, to departing guests. The legend is that a single woman who takes the groom's cake home and sleeps with it beneath her pillow will dream of the man she will someday marry. A groom's cake is a completely optional item. Many couples bypass the tradition.

ORDERING THE CAKE(S)

Plan to put down a deposit; ask to have the order put in writing, and keep a copy for your records. Make sure the order form specifies not only the final cost, but also all your selections with regard to flavor, filling, topping, shape, size, decorations, and delivery time. You will also want to confirm in writing exactly how and where the cake will be delivered or picked up.

> It is a tradition to wrap and freeze a piece of the wedding cake (usually the small top layer, if the cake is tiered). This is later unwrapped and eaten by the bride and groom on the occasion of their first anniversary.

Cakes on page 161 top right-hand corner and page 162 bottom left-hand corner courtesy of Paula Cutone.

Who can give law to lovers? Love is a greater law to itself. —BOETHIUS

Baker Worksheet

Bakery/baker:

Address:

Phone: _____ Hours:

Appointment date & time:

Date & amount of deposit:

Date & amount of balance due:

Date & time of delivery or pickup:

Location of delivery or pickup:

Terms of cancellation:

Notes:

Wedding Cake Worksheet

Element of cake   Description

    Size of cake

    Shape of cake

    Number of tiers

    Number cake will serve

    Flavor of cake

    Flavor of filling

    Flavor of icing

    Icing decorations

    Cake top

    Cake decorations

    Other

    Groom's cake

        Flavor

        Icing

    Number will serve

    Shape and size

    Top

    Decorations

    Other

Cake Expenses Worksheet

	Cost
Wedding cake	
Cake decorations	....
Cake top	....
Groom's cake	
Cake decorations	....
Cake top	....
Groom's cake boxes	....
Cake knife	....
Cake table	....
Cake table covering	....
Delivery	....
Other	
....	....
....	....
....	....
....	....
....	....
....	....
....	....
....	....
....	....
Total	....

Chapter Seventeen: The Reception Schedule

Many brides think of the reception as the part of the day when they really get to display the new couple's style. A lot of planning goes into conveying just the right "feel" at the party. And why not? You will want your guests to enjoy all the marvelous food, festive decorations, and lively music you have selected.

To make your planning easier, the traditional sequence of events for a reception is examined in detail in this chapter. Of course, you may choose to omit or adapt any of these steps to fit your own style and budget.

TRADITIONAL SEQUENCE OF RECEPTION EVENTS

1. Reception line
2. Mingling/cocktails
3. Guests are officially seated
4. Bride, groom, and wedding party are announced
5. Blessing by the officiant
6. Toast by the best man
7. Food service begins
8. Newlyweds' first dance
9. Dessert
10. Cutting of the cake
11. Throwing of the bouquet and garter
12. Newlyweds' farewell dance

Before you do anything...

Before things really get started at the reception, it is a good idea to give your photographer a few moments at the conclusion of the ceremony to take some of the group photos on his list. (See the chapter on photography for a suggested shot list.) These poses will include the entire wedding party, specific family groups, and any friends you feel should be included in the photo record.

Since you won't want your guests to wait too long, you should make a

love is the whole and more than all —e.e. cummings

point of telling all the attendants that they will be needed for photos immediately after the ceremony. (It is also advisable to "scout" your facility ahead of time so you can direct people to a spot where they can freshen up.)

The receiving line

This is a formality, although most couples find it to be a very pleasant one.

You will have a good deal of flexibility in setting up your receiving line. Some couples hold it at the wedding site, before the reception itself begins. Others dispense with it entirely. This is certainly an acceptable option; if you and your fiance are more comfortable simply circulating at the reception to meet the guests at their tables, you should feel free to do so.

Note that your guests will probably arrive at the reception location before you have a chance to greet them formally. You might arrange for suitable background music to make the wait less awkward. For a very large number of guests, consider an additional setting of light snacks exclusively for the period before your arrival.

Here is the traditional order of the receiving line. It can be altered or adapted as needed; it is not at all uncommon, for instance, to include other relatives or close friends in the line.

> *(From left to right)*
> Bride's mother
> Bride's father (optional; he may be occupied elsewhere as host of the
> reception)
> Groom's mother
> Groom's father
> Bride
> Groom
> Maid of honor
> Bridesmaids (optional)

Traditionally, the bride's mother is at the head of the line because of her role as the hostess.

Helpful hint: set the line up in a place with ample room that is unlikely to disturb the normal traffic patterns of the party. Also, try to keep conversations short as a courtesy to the guests waiting in line to greet you.

I sleep, but my heart is awake. Listen!
My beloved is knocking. —SONG OF SONGS 4:2 (NEW ENGLISH BIBLE)

Mingling/cocktails

After the receiving line, it is customary to allow some time for the guests to chat and have a drink or two. This is an excellent time for the photographer to take candid shots.

Guests are seated

The host should inform the guests that it is time to be seated without making them feel rushed.

An organized seating plan will help keep confusion to a minimum. If you decide to assign each guest a seat, you will need place cards (available through your stationer). Place cards should be arranged on a table in such a way that guests can see the names and table numbers from a good distance.

Announcement of the bride and groom

The host usually introduces the bride and groom by saying something like, "May I present to you, for the first time, Mr. and Mrs. John Smith!" This announcement can be accompanied by fanfare and/or a drum roll if you wish.

The host then announces the members of the wedding party individually, usually with each usher escorting a bridesmaid. Since your family and friends may not know the attendants, you may wish to prepare a brief personalized description for each member of the wedding party (two to three sentences maximum).

Blessing

The officiant of the wedding ceremony is usually invited to participate in the festivities afterwards. If he is agreeable to doing so, he may bless the meal at this time; he may also bless the couple and invite the guests to join him in prayer for the newlyweds, their families, and the entire gathering.

Love like ours can never die! —RUDYARD KIPLING

Toast by the best man

At this time, it is appropriate for the best man to propose a toast to the newlyweds. It should be well-rehearsed, tasteful, meaningful, and concise. The best man may also propose a toast to the newlyweds' families, particularly their parents. (Other toasts, such as those made by the father of the bride and/or groom, may also be made at this time.)

Food service

This will usually be either a sit-down or a buffet meal, depending on your arrangements.

Newlyweds' first dance

This is perhaps the most romantic moment of the reception. It is customary to allow the new couple to take to the dance floor before any of the guests, and for this dance to be followed by the bride's dance with her father. Any other "special" dances that are to be incorporated into the festivities should take place before the rest of the guests take to the dance floor.

Dessert

You can plan to have dessert in your menu with your caterer or food service, or serve cake to your guests as dessert.

Cutting of the cake

The cutting of the cake is a special moment; you will want to be sure your photographer is on hand to record it.

It is customary for the bride to place her left hand over the groom's right hand as the cake is cut; this allows for a nice shot of both rings. Another popular picture is one of the two of you feeding each other cake.

Note: Your guests should be served cake at their tables; otherwise, the crowding may keep everyone from getting a piece. One nice approach is to have

Love makes those young whom age doth chill,
And whom he finds young, keeps young still —WILLIAM CARTWRIGHT

the bridesmaids team up with the ushers to serve the cake. (This gives the attendants a chance to mix with the guests.)

Throwing of the bouquet and garter

Many brides ask for a smaller additional bouquet and throw this, reserving the more elaborate one so it can be preserved.

As we have noted earlier, each of these rituals is optional. The throwing of the garter is a crowd pleaser, but don't do it if it makes you uncomfortable.

Newlyweds' farewell dance

If you plan to make a grand exit, do so right after your farewell dance.

It is considered good etiquette for the guests to remain at the reception until the newlyweds leave. If you plan to stay late at the reception, be sure to inform the guests of this, so they feel no obligation to leave after you do.

TIPS ON MAKING YOUR RECEPTION RUN SMOOTHLY

Host or hostess. If your reception is to include a large number of guests, you might want to consider designating a host or hostess. This person might be someone close to you or your family; alternatively, the reception facility may be able to provide you with someone to fulfill this role. The host or hostess should be dynamic, willing to take charge, and capable of moving things along smoothly. (This may be just the spot for that relative who loves to be the center of attention!)

If you are planning a very large reception and want to include your parents or your groom's parents as hosts, remember that it will be very difficult for them to relax under such circumstances. Another person may be able to coordinate the events perfectly, yet still recognize your parents as the "official" hosts.

Directions. If the reception and ceremony are to be held at separate locations, you will need to provide good directions. One way is to include them in the ceremony program. This will eliminate the possibility of guests losing their directions before the wedding day. Alternatively, you may opt to have the ushers hand out directions to the guests as they leave the wedding location.

Many waters cannot quench love;
no flood can sweep it away. —SONG OF SONGS 8:7 (NEW ENGLISH BIBLE)

Gifts and cards. Many guests will bring gifts to your reception. A beautifully decorated gift table will draw attention and encourage people to leave gifts in one centralized location.

A decorated keepsake box or basket for wedding cards is also a good idea. You will want to assign someone to take charge of the card box or basket, both for reasons of security (many of the envelopes will contain cash or checks) and to direct guests as to where the cards should be left.

Some advice on tipping

There are a number of service people you will want to tip at the reception; here is a brief summary of the customary approaches. Of course, you should feel free to use your own judgment with regard to tipping.

It is generally the host of the reception who tips for the services.

Food service/hotel/restaurant/hall. Plan to tip appropriate amounts at your discretion:

Caterer
Hotel banquet manager
Restaurant manager
Bridal consultant
Hall manager

(Also: note that a fifteen to twenty percent tip on the reception bill is customarily distributed among waiters, waitresses, and bartenders.)

Hotel/restaurant/hall attendants. Plan to tip at fifty cents per guest (or prearranged sum):

Coat room attendant
Powder room attendant

Drivers. Plan to tip fifteen to twenty percent of transportation costs.

Note: Photographers, bakers, florists, and musicians are generally not tipped unless they provide exceptional service or special help with the reception.

An 'twere offered as I should elect, I had rather marry to a state of concord than be born to a state of nobility. —THOMAS, DUKE OF CLARENCE

Reception Events Worksheet

Host/hostess: _____

Address: _____

Phone: _____

Order of the Receiving Line

1. _____	21. _____
2. _____	22. _____
3. _____	23. _____
4. _____	24. _____
5. _____	25. _____
6. _____	26. _____
7. _____	27. _____
8. _____	28. _____
9. _____	29. _____
10. _____	30. _____
11. _____	31. _____
12. _____	32. _____
13. _____	33. _____
14. _____	34. _____
15. _____	35. _____
16. _____	36. _____
17. _____	37. _____
18. _____	38. _____
19. _____	39. _____
20. _____	40. _____

Schedule of Reception Events

Event	Time
Receiving line	....
Seating of the guests	....
Announcement of the newlyweds and the wedding party	....
Blessing	....
Toasts	....
Food service	....
Newlyweds' first dance	....
Dessert	....
Cutting of the cake	....
Throwing of the bouquet / garter	....
Newlyweds' farewell dance	....
Other special events	
....	....
....	....
....	....
....	....
....	....
....	....
....	....
....	....
....	....

Honeymoon

Chapter Eighteen: The Honeymoon

Congratulations!

As you and your partner begin your new life together as man and wife, you will look back on your wedding day with a great deal of fondness. There will be some beautiful memories . . . but there are more to come!

We have reproduced in this chapter a list of the most popular destinations for newlyweds; perhaps you'll come across something that seems perfect for you. In addition, your travel agent will be able to provide you with plenty of informative magazines and circulars. Whether your fantasy is relaxing on a tropical beach or touring the great cities of the world, it probably won't be long before you find a destination that will match your tastes and your budget.

Once you have decided upon a location, shop around. Package prices can vary widely among travel agents. You should be prepared to make your plans well in advance, and to pay for your tickets or package deal four to six weeks before the honeymoon.

Suggested honeymoon destinations

Canada
>   Banff National Park, Alberta
>   Calgary, Alberta
>   Halifax, Nova Scotia
>   Montreal, Quebec
>   Toronto, Ontario
>   Prince Edward Island
>   St. John's, Newfoundland

Caribbean
>   Aruba
>   Cayman Islands
>   Little Dix Bay, British Virgin Islands
>   Montego Bay, Jamaica
>   Nassau, Bahamas
>   Negril, Jamaica

The pleasure of love is in loving. —FRANCOIS, DUC DE LA ROCHEFOUCALD

Ocho Rios, Jamaica
Paradise Island, Bahamas
St. Croix

Europe

Athens, Greece
Barcelona, Spain
London, England
Paris, France
Rome, Italy
Venice, Italy

Mexico

Baja California region
Cancun, Quintana Roo
Guadalajara, Jalisco
Isla de Cozumel, Quintana Roo
Puerto Vallarta, Jalisco

South Pacific

The Marquesas
Tahiti

United States

Arizona (Grand Canyon National Park)
California (Popular scenic touring route: the Pacific Coast
    Highway)
Disneyland (Anaheim, California)
Walt Disney World (Orlando, Florida)
Hawaii (Popular island destinations: Maui; Kauai; Oahu)
Massachusetts (Popular summer destination: Cape Cod)
New York State (Popular destination: Niagara Falls)
South Carolina (Popular destination: Hilton Head)
Pennsylvania (Popular destination: Poconos)
Puerto Rico (Popular destination: San Juan)
U.S. Virgin Islands (Popular destination: Caneel Bay)

How blessed to be loved! How much more blessed to be able to love! —ANONYMOUS

Honeymoon Worksheet

Destination: _____

Carrier: _____

Dates: _____

Itinerary: _____

Notes: _____

_____

_____

Destination: _____

Carrier: _____

Dates: _____

Itinerary: _____

Notes: _____

_____

_____

Destination: _____

Carrier: _____

Dates: _____

Itinerary: _____

Notes: _____

_____

_____

_____

Items to Take on Honeymoon